RESURRECTING
KENNEDY

RESURRECTING KENNEDY

JUDGE HAL MOROZ

NEW YORK   ATLANTA   WASHINGTON   BOSTON

Resurrecting Kennedy

Judge Hal Moroz

Access to the public addresses and statements of our 35th President of the United States is available through a wide range of sources in the public domain.
The author of this work wishes to acknowledge the outstanding archives of the John F. Kennedy Presidential Library and Museum, Columbia Point
Boston, Massachusetts 02125

The author of this work also wishes to acknowledge the exceptionally outstanding archives of The Ronald Reagan Presidential Foundation located in Simi Valley, California.
The author is a member of the Foundation, and encourages everyone interested in supporting and preserving the legacy of President Ronald Reagan to join the Foundation.
Membership can be obtained by writing The Ronald Reagan Presidential Foundation, 40 Presidential Drive, Simi Valley, California 93065, or via the internet at
www.reaganfoundation.org.

Unless otherwise noted, Scripture quotations are from
The King James Version of the Bible.

The opinions expressed in this book are solely the opinions of the author and do not necessarily reflect the opinions of any individual, groups,
organizations or business entities mentioned herein.
The quotes, selected writings, and articles contained in this book are reprinted with permission or are permissible for use under existing law.

Printed in the United States of America

"The cost of freedom is always high, and Americans
have always paid it. And one path we shall never choose,
and that is the path of surrender or submission.
Our goal is not the victory of might, but the vindication of right.
Not peace at the expense of freedom, but both peace and freedom,
here in this hemisphere, and, we hope, around the world.
God willing, that goal will be achieved."

~ President John F. Kennedy
Cuban Missile Crisis Address, October 22, 1962

RESURRECTING KENNEDY

Contents

Introduction

Defending Freedom

"In the long history of the world,
only a few generations have been granted the role of
defending freedom in its hour of maximum danger.
I do not shrink from this responsibility—I welcome it."

~ President John F. Kennedy
January 20, 1961

John Fitzgerald Kennedy is undoubtedly one of the most enduring and beloved political figures of our time. Charismatic, handsome, a master of the spoken word, and the first chief executive to use television as his bully pulpit, Kennedy was a leader! He inspired a new generation of Americans to reach for the stars, and so we do. JFK ushered in a rebirth of the days of Camelot, with all the majesty and charm of that era.

JFK embodied youth and achievement: a war hero, a congressman, a senator, and finally president. He was the personification of the American Spirit! The youngest man to be elected president at age 43, President Kennedy was a Commander in Chief who believed in employing unconventional forces to achieve political objectives – Vietnam being one case in point – and the architect of a competitive America that could overtake the Soviet Union in the space race, and set a goal of landing a man on the moon and returning him safely back to the earth. He set the goal, and we did it! He dreamed great dreams, and inspired us to achieve them, even if they were not during his lifetime.

President Kennedy's life and presidency came to an abrupt end on November 22, 1963, after an assassin's bullets mortally wounded him in Dallas. He was struck down at the height of his political and military success. And each anniversary of his assassination is immortalized by our national and world media. His death is shrouded in mystery and notions of conspiracy, but this is not the legacy of John F. Kennedy.

President Kennedy is one of the most enduring political figures of our time for a reason. His words and vision inspired America! They are his legacy. This is why I wrote and edited this work: To resurrect the truly American ideals of this great man. He was not perfect, not by a long shot, but he understood and championed those American values and ideals that made us a great nation. And as Philippians 4:8[1] commands, I will dwell on the good. His belief in God and the enduring American Spirit made us believe all things were possible ... and indeed with God they truly are!

This work is a tribute to the man and his words that inspired a generation of Americans --- and many more to come! JFK has a message for the confused and huddled masses yearning for real political leadership, who wonder what it means to really be

---

[1] Philippians 4:8 – "Finally, brethren, whatsoever things are true, whatsoever things are honest, whatsoever things are just, whatsoever things are pure, whatsoever things are lovely, whatsoever things are of good report; if there be any virtue, and if there be any praise, think on these things."

American. There are valuable lessons in his powerful words. And they are sure to stir the heart, and bring to mind those treasured, good memories of yesteryear, and inspire a new generation of Americans to be all they can be!

John F. Kennedy's key speeches are documented in this work, a priceless collection of selected thoughts and utterances of a man who changed the course of American history, and articulated the way forward for this last best hope of man on earth. This is his legacy, one worth resurrecting and studying by this generation, and the generations of Americans to come.

~ Judge Hal Moroz

~ * ~

"I do not believe in a fate that will fall on us no matter what we do. I do believe in a fate that will fall on us if we do nothing. So, with all the creative energy at our command, let us begin an era of national renewal. Let us renew our determination, our courage, and our strength. And let us renew our faith and our hope.

"We have every right to dream heroic dreams. Those who say that we are in a time when there are no heroes just don't know where to look. You can see heroes every day going in and out of factory gates. Others, a handful in number, produce enough food to feed all of us and then the world beyond. You meet heroes across a counter -- and they are on both sides of that counter. There are entrepreneurs with faith in themselves and faith in an idea who create new jobs, new wealth and opportunity. They are individuals and families whose taxes support the government and whose voluntary gifts support church, charity, culture, art, and education. Their patriotism is quiet but deep. Their values sustain our national life.

"I have used the words 'they' and 'their' in speaking of these heroes. I could say 'you' and 'your' because I am addressing the heroes of whom I speak -- you, the citizens of this blessed land. Your dreams, your hopes, your goals are going to be the dreams, the hopes, and the goals of this administration, so help me God."

~ President Ronald Reagan
Inaugural Address, January 20, 1981

The Journey

The American Legion Post Speech

November 11, 1945

Crosscup-Pishon American Legion Post, Boston, Massachusetts

Our foreign policy today may well determine the kind of life we will live here for generations. For the peace and prosperity of this country are truly indivisible from the peace and prosperity of the world in this atomic age.

But before we whole-heartedly subscribe to any foreign policy, it may be well for us to examine the kinds of government that are taking over in the countries of post-war Europe and try to estimate where they are headed. I would like to offer for your consideration today my personal observations on three of these countries— England, Ireland, and Germany—victor, neutral, and vanquished.

The subject is a very broad one so that I am going to speak chiefly on the political parties of England and Ireland to try to estimate the reasons for their success or failure and to study the problems they face and their prospects for the future. In the case of Germany I merely propose to estimate the possibilities as they appear at the present time of building any kind of democratic government— democratic in the western sense.

The outstanding political event of the year was the emergence of the Labour Party in England as the majority party for the first time in history. Their overwhelming victory came as a surprise to everyone including themselves. Even Professor Laski, whose views on one thing and another have been pouring into the United States during the last three months, told me that he only expected to win by fifty seats, and he said it as though he himself really didn't believe it. I think what threw most prognostications off was the amazing popularity of Mr. Churchill. This popularity was general not only in the Conservative Party but in the Labour Party itself. I attended dozens of Labour Party rallies and I didn't hear a single speech which does not contain a tribute to Mr. Churchill for his notable work during the war. They cheered him and then they voted against him. Why?

I think first and foremost because the Conservative Party had been in power during the most difficult times in English history, both at home and abroad. The Conservative Party was the majority party during the years of the depression when poverty stalked the Midlands and the coal fields of Wales, and thousands and thousands lived off the meager pittance of the dole. Where Roosevelt made his political reputation by his treatment of the depression, the Conservative Party lost theirs.

Later the Conservative Party was the party in power during the days of appeasement, when crises followed crises, and Germany slowly and inexorably spread over the face of Europe. Few seemed to remember that the opposition of the Labor Party to this policy of appeasement consisted principally of voting against armaments and conscription. The Conservatives were in power and they had the responsibility. And finally when the fiasco in Norway brought the end to the rule of Mr. Chamberlain, the Coalition government took over and all parties therefore shared in the successes of the next five years which culminated in victory.

Thus the Conservative government was stained with two awful and tragic periods in English history. That the Conservatives realized that their name was a liability was tacitly confessed when they changed their name to the National Party during this last election.

The second contributing factor to the defeat of the Conservative Party was that England traditionally has been a country with tremendous contrasts between the very rich and the very poor.

That arch Tory, Benjamin Disraeli, Earl of Beaconsfield, once stated that England was divided into two nations—the rich and the poor.

With the turnover caused by the war, the contribution made by the poor as well as the rich, the coming of the American troops with their high pay, with their stories of cars, refrigerators, and radios for all, a new spirit—a new restlessness—and a fresh desire for the better things of life had become strong in Britain.

The third reason for the Conservative defeat was that Labour made the most of the fact that it never had held office. It was relatively easy, therefore, to be all things to all men. With higher wages and shorter hours, happy days would be here again. They attacked the Conservatives' pre-war foreign policy—attacked government by a privileged class. The day of the working-man was to be at hand— and to the Socialists, virtually everyone was a working-man.

All these arguments which were put forward with vigor and cleverness had their effect. The Conservative Party, fat and happy with years of victory, let their political ace, Mr. Churchill, carry the ball.

Instead of a vigorous campaign on the virtues of private enterprise, they offered a watered down version of blood, sweat, and tears for the years of peace. Blood, sweat, and tears was fitted to the desperate days of 1940 but not to 1945 to a people whose chronic fatigue and exhaustion had brought them to a sharp-tempered dissatisfaction with life in England.

The result was, therefore, inevitable, although few could see it. The victory was overwhelming. Labour with its far-reaching plan for Socialization and for "the new foreign policy" swept into office.

What are the prospects in store for the Labour Party? She faces tremendous problems both at home and abroad. Most serious is Britain's financial problem.

Ernest Bevin once said, "Britain is an island of coal surrounded by fish." Only by the most vigorous governmental regulations in the war was she able to grow as much as two-thirds of her food. She must import not only food but iron and oil and most of the other raw materials with which she supports her daily life.

Before the war she had three sources of income to pay for these imports: the money derived from goods sold abroad, the interest from investments overseas, and receipts from shipping services.

But during this war, she sold most of her overseas investments, her shipping future is precarious and depends on our policy on the sea, and thus, her export trade must carry a tremendous burden.

England must build up her export trade to six times what it was in 1944 and three times what it was in the normal year of 1938 to make both ends meet.

But if she concentrates on manufacturing for the export trade, the people at home will suffer, and if she builds for the people at home, it will be bad medicine financially for England—and in the long run, fatal. This is the great problem facing Labour in England today.

I have stressed today the politics and economics of Great Britain more than her foreign situation. I have done this because Mr. Bevin's recent speech proved how right Benjamin Disraeli was when he defined a Tory as a Whig in power. Responsibility is a very sobering thing. Although Mr. Laski may talk about the new foreign policy of Socialism, Britain stands today as Britain has always stood—for the empire. Britain's relations with the countries of Europe and Asia will not be substantially different than they have ever been.

I propose today to discuss one of these countries—Ireland—because I think its relationship with England is typical of the many problems which England will be facing in the future with increasing regularity.

The world's attention was turned to Ireland last July by a debate in the Irish Dail between Prime Minister DeValera and Mr. James Dillon. For when Mr. DeValera answered Mr. Dillon's question concerning Eire's constitutional status with the words, "We are a Republic," it immediately raised the question of whether or not Eire was a member of the British Commonwealth of nations, the connecting link of which is a common allegiance to the British crown.

Mr. DeValera waited a week before he answered this question. The world waited with him. When the answer finally came, it left many observers somewhat bewildered, but it neatly extracted Mr. DeValera from a very precarious political position. He did not say whether or not he believed that Eire was a member of the British Commonwealth of nations. He merely quoted a British statement of 1931 to the effect that she was—and left it at that. Why these careful words, this guarded reply after a week of study?

Behind the debate of Mr. Dillon and Mr. DeValera loomed the fundamental problem behind all Irish politics—the problem of ending the partition, which divides the twenty-six counties of the south, which form Eire, and the six counties of the north known as Ulster which are attached directly to Great Britain. That this partition must be ended both Mr. DeValera and Mr. Dillon agree. On this all Irishmen agree. The dispute lies in the method to be followed.

A great many people in Eire feel that the only way to end partition is to come to an agreement with the British, to take a full part in the British Commonwealth of nations, and to make a treaty of mutual defense. They argue that the British will not tolerate a sullen neutral on their vulnerable western flank. Rather than have this, the British will support the government in Ulster until the end of time. This is the view of the Fine Gael or United Ireland Party formerly led by Cosgrave and now by that able warrior who proved his toughness in the wars against the black and tans, General Mulcahy.

The day that I called on General Mulcahy he was sitting in a small office surrounded by books, but he looked like the soldier he was. He was a man of strong opinions. When an Irish politician gives you his views on his country's position, you know that they are not lightly held and that he was probably shed some blood in their defense. The most impressive object in General Mulcahy's room is a large picture of Michael Collins. We spent only a few minutes talking about the General and several hours talking about Collins.

This young man who was killed in his early thirties looms as large today in Ireland as when he died. As General Mulcahy said, "If Michael Collins had lived, the history of Ireland would be different." Collins, who died in the Civil War of 1922, was only one of the many brilliant young Irishmen who died in what Kevin O'Higgins called, "the spilling of the wine."

But against the party of General Mulcahy is ranged the powerful Fianna Fail "Soldiers of Ireland" which now holds a majority in the Irish Dail. This is the party of DeValera who fought Cosgrave and Collins in 1922 until finally defeated and who now continues the battle in the Dail. These are the men who claim that everything that Ireland has ever gotten from England has been only at the end of a long and bitter struggle. Always it has been too little and too late. This is the party of DeValera, and in his government he is surrounded by men of the same tough fiber. All have been in British and Irish prisons and many of them have wounds which still ache when the cold rains come in from the west.

One of these is Frank Gallagher, DeValera's secretary. Instead of the hundreds and hundreds of young men who work in our OWI and in the British Ministry of Information, in Eire there is just one man, Gallagher, and he is a gold mine of information. He has been with DeValera for many years and fought in the war against the British and in the Civil War. One evening when I had been talking with him for hours, I said, "Frank, I think I'm taking up too much of your time."

He replied, "My boy, I have the best job in the world. I am the only man in Ireland who gets paid for just talking."

Mr. Dillon, an independent who supports the opposition to Mr. DeValera, was attempting to demonstrate in his debate with DeValera that Eire's constitutional position was, as he put it, "like that of a cat which has its tail caught in the door—neither in nor out—and in a state of considerable intellectual perplexity."

He feels that Eire today is bound to England with the closest of economic bonds. England today buys more than 90 per cent of Eire's exports. England also owes Eire over 400,000,000 pounds sterling, which makes Eire one of the wealthiest nations proportionately in the world. This balance was built up during the war when Eire supplied Britain with food on credit.

Economically and strategically, Eire is bound to England, argues Mr. Dillon. It is only nursing ancient quarrels long since dead for Mr. DeValera to consistently hold to his position that he will make no commitments of any nature until Ireland is united under the flag of Eire.

But at the present time DeValera holds the whip hand.

The Irish are as vigorous in their support of DeValera's policy of neutrality as they are proud of the thousands and thousands of young men who left their country to join the British army. And to those critics who wonder whether the Irish are getting soft, they point to the seven Victoria Crosses, England's highest decoration, won by soldiers from the Southern counties. They take singular pleasure in the fact that in spite of their close ties to England, they were none won by the soldiers from Ulster.

DeValera has a unique hold on the hearts of the Irish people. The fact that it was DeValera who made the deal that returned the now famous ports of Berehaven, Queenstown, and Lough Swilly to Eire gives them confidence that it will be DeValera who will finally settle the problem of Partition. He has always won support for his policies by appealing to the strong patriotic instinct of all Irishmen. Thus he won support for his policy of neutrality during the war by identifying neutrality with freedom from England, which will always win support.

There is no compromise in DeValera's firm, ascetic face. He has a passionate intensity and single-mindedness in the course he is taking that brooks no opposition. He is extremely conscious that his visit to the German Legation on Hitler's death caused unfavorable comment in America. He discussed it with me at some length. He was determined to carry out Eire's policy of strict neutrality to the end, and carry it out he did. To all critics he answers, "I kept Ireland out of the war."

Eire at the present time has a unique political set-up. There is no "left" party in the accepted sense. The "left" in Eire are not those who favor more and more governmental control as in France for example, but are those who favor a complete break with England; the right—those who believe in working with England in the Commonwealth. DeValera walks a tightrope between the two extremes. While in his heart he is far to the Left, yet he realizes that economically and strategically Eire is bound by the strongest ties to England and that only with England's support can Partition be ended. His vague answer to Mr. Dillon's question about Ireland's position in the British Commonwealth, in the debate referred to before, clearly demonstrates his delicate position.

As to the possibility of his ending Partition, no one can say. Sir Alan Brooke, head of the government in Ulster, recently roared down to the gentleman in Dublin that "not an inch" will he give up of the six counties of the North. And it is somewhat dubious if England, after its narrow escape during this conflict, will ever consent to giving up her naval base at Belfast until she at least has assurances of support in case of another war. Some people feel that General Mulcahy and Mr. Dillon, with their willingness to play a full part in the British Commonwealth, may yet be the ones to end Partition.

We have discussed today a country, England, with two political parties, Conservative and Labour, split over the extent of government control of industry. We have discussed another country, Ireland, with its two great political parties, the Fine Gael and the Fianna Fail which are divided, not over economic policies, but over the extent of their country's cooperation with England.

We turn now to a third country, Germany, whose geographic, economic, and political structure have been smashed by war and the subsequent peace. In order to estimate the possibilities of Germany building out of its present ruin any democratic parties in which the Western allies can place confidence, let us look at Germany today.

Germany is now split into four divisions, the eastern section under Russia, the northwest under the British, the west along the Rhine valley under the French, and the southwest under the United States. Its capitol and greatest city, Berlin, is similarly divided and is likewise administered by a council composed of representatives of each of the four allied nations.

Berlin today is a gutted ruin. Its destruction far surpassed anything that I had ever imagined. The buildings which still stand are merely shells, and where the three million people who still remain in Berlin live, is a mystery. The streets are filled with them—their faces colorless, their lips a pale tan, their expressions lifeless and dead, as though they were suffering from shock. Occasionally, and it appears incongruous, you see a dog. They won't last through this winter. The streets are swarmed with Russian soldiers who look young and stocky and tough, and grim and dirty. They regard American equipment with the greatest respect and they say that even Marshall Zhukov's eyes popped during a victory parade in Berlin when the Second Armored "Hell-on-Wheels" Division came by with its miles of the newest equipment and its rugged and perfectly disciplined troops.

The food problem is more acute in Berlin than anywhere else in Germany. The average ration runs to about twelve hundred calories, which is below the subsistence level. The city of Berlin is being administered as a single unit, and all the citizens—no matter in which section—get the same ration. The reason for this is obvious. If the United States fed their 700,000 people better than the Russians, for example, fed theirs, hungry Berliners would swarm into the American zone. Everyone in Berlin is therefore treated alike.

The Russians have not only sent back all the food and machinery which they can move to Russia, but they are transporting nearly all the able-bodied Germans between the ages of 15 and 60 to Russia as laborers.

As far as the Americans and Russians getting along in Berlin, though there was some suspicion at first, relations now seem to be reasonably cordial. The Russians acted with far greater speed than we in opening the schools, starting newspapers, and permitting political parties to function—as long as they have the right politics. But the Russians have a long way to go before they win much support from the German people. The Russian army that first entered Berlin was a fighting army and it acted with great violence. Many Germans who might have been Communist sympathizers were thus alienated.

In the western cities like Bremen, Frankfurt, and Salzburg, the people have been living very well up to now. They have had food reserves to supplement their low ration, but by winter these rations will be gone and they will be on a bare subsistence level. There will be no coal, and many of their houses have been destroyed. The Germans this winter will pay for their support of Hitler.

Our occupation troops are as fine as any I ever saw. I watched an inspection by General Eisenhower of several thousand troops in Frankfurt. They were rugged looking and their discipline was perfect, but it remained for a Marine Major with whom I was standing to give the final accolade, "Why," he said, with astonishment, "they look like Marines!"

What is the future of Germany? Some people believe that Germany should be split up into principalities or divided into zones of control as she is now. The objection to this solution, as Bismarck realized, is that Germany forms a geographical and economic unit. British-occupied Germany is only 40 per cent self-sufficient in food—ours only 70 per cent, and while the Russian zone is 100 per cent self-sufficient in food, it is short on coal and iron, the supplies of which are under French control in the Ruhr valley.

Others say leave the Germans alone to work out their own salvation, they are too weak to ever menace us again. But Germany is in no position to build any kind of democratic government, and I do not think that it is particularly desirable for the United States to leave Germany a political vacuum which the Russians might be only too glad to fill. I believe that we should keep some measure of control indefinitely in Germany. The German people will never forget nor forgive this defeat. The French did not in 1870, and whether Nazi or anti-Nazi, there is no reason to believe the Germans will after their defeat in 1945. Their scientific experiments particularly must be carefully supervised, because science is fast learning the secret of annihilation.

I have spoken today of three countries—England, Ireland, and Germany. All these countries are different and all face different problems. But from each one, and indeed from every country that I visited in Europe, I came away with one great impression—the greatness of my own country, America. Unless he has been abroad since the war ended, no American can possibly realize what a tremendous place America occupies in the world today. In England, for example, before the war, an American was just a tourist and America the land where the tourist came from. When I was in Russia in 1939, Americans were viewed with darkest suspicion and considerable dislike.

But now a change has come about. All of our millions of young men who swarmed over Europe, all the millions and millions of tons of equipment that were poured by us into the war has made Europeans realize that here, indeed, is the great productive giant of the world.

During this war we fought on two fronts, and at the same time shipped 41 billion dollars worth of lend-lease equipment abroad for the use of other countries. No other country in the world could have ever duplicated this tremendous job. We occupy a great position in the world today. We must measure up to our responsibility.

But we must not forget that we have here in our own country a problem just as great as that of any other country in the world. And that is the problem of keeping our great productive machinery going at full capacity. We must do this if we are going to provide jobs for all those young men who are coming home. This is the first and most important task we face. We will be in a far better position to help solve the world's problems if we have first solved our own.

The Commencement Address

June 3, 1955

Assumption College, Worcester, Massachusetts

This is my first visit to Massachusetts in over nine months - my first speech in nearly a year. It is, thus, a pleasure as well as an honor to be here today at Assumption College.

I saw Assumption College for the first time on the afternoon of June 10th, twenty-four hours after disaster had struck from the West. No institution could have suffered the losses that Assumption suffered that day and survived if there was not in the minds of those in positions of responsibility an overriding scene of the function and need of such a College.

The disaster of two years ago was not in any sense a blessing in disguise, but it did give all of us an opportunity to reassess the purposes for which the school has developed. That that re-evaluation has reaffirmed the importance of this College to us all can be seen in the wide-spread support that has been given from all groups in Assumption's struggle to survive. To Bishop Wright, to Father Desautels, the Faculty, the Student Body and the Alumni, this Community and State owes a special obligation. The ultimate result will be that Assumption will play an even larger role in the life of New England than it has in the past.

It is highly important that this should be so. Assumption College in these critical days has a threefold function. Its primary end, in the words of Pope Pius XI, is "preparing man for what he must be and do here below, in order to attain the sublime end for which he was created," the perfection of man through the proper development of all his faculties in the light of his supernatural end. In addition, the Catholic College, since it is a College, must be concerned not only with the student's spiritual development but also his intellectual development. Assumption College has recognized that its students, in the words of Jacques Maritain, "in order to reach self-determination, for which he is made, *** needs discipline and tradition, which will both weigh heavily on him and strengthen him."

Secondly, Assumption has a special responsibility imposed upon it because it represents one of the major channels connecting the United States with the great sea of France's religious, cultural and social traditions. What is most striking in the French tradition is its extraordinary vitality. Many countries have had a brief golden age. France's has existed from before the Renaissance to the present day.

We can trace the continuity of French Art from the stained glass windows at Chartres to Rouault today. We can trace the continuity of French painting from the Avignon Pieta to Matisse's Chapel at Venice: French literature flows like a torrent from the song of Roland to Paul Claudel. We can trace the continuity of French missionary zeal from the founding of the Association for the Propagation of the Faith in Lyons in the 12th century to Assumption College in Worcester in the 20th.

Indeed, it is three Frenchmen today who have stimulated the rebirth of Catholic intellectual life: Jacques Maritain, our outstanding Catholic philosopher - Francois Mauriac, our outstanding Catholic writer - Paul Claudel, our outstanding Catholic poet. This is the matchless tradition, that it is the role of Assumption through its graduates to interpret for America.

We are fortunate in New England where Americans of French and Canadian extraction play such a major role that here at Assumption College we should have the means of maintaining such a close tie with so much that is important and so little known. As Bishop Wright said several years ago, God "has brought you here and gave you the force and grace and the vision to retain your traditions of language and culture in order that you might *** interpret to us the wisdom of French speaking christendom in a moment of history which English speaking christendom and all the English speaking world needed so badly." This College serves as a wellspring from which all of us may gather direction and inspiration: You who graduate can share with us the French speaking world's tradition and wisdom in a period of disintegration.

And lastly, Assumption has the function common to all universities, the continuing search for the truth, both for its own sake and because only if we possess it can we really be free. Never has the task of finding the truth been more difficult. In a struggle between modern states "truth" has become a weapon in the battle of power - it is bent, twisted and subverted to fit the pattern of national policy. Frequently, we in the West feel ourselves forced by this drum beat of lies and propaganda to be "discriminating" in our selection of what facets of the truth we ourselves will disclose. Thus, the responsibility of a free university to pursue its own objective studies is even more important today than ever before. Assumption College has succeeded in carrying out this mission, so that today it stands as a bulwark on the North American continent in the battle for the preservation of Christian civilization.

I say this and not because I believe Christianity is a weapon in the present world struggle, but because I believe religion itself is at the root of the struggle, not in terms of the physical organizations of Christianity versus those of Atheism, but in terms of Good versus Evil, right versus wrong, in terms of "the stern encounter" of which Cardinal Newman so prophetically wrote:

"Then will come the stern encounter when two real and living principles, simple, entire, and consistent, one in the church and the other out of it, at length rush upon one another contending nor for names and words or half views, but for elementary notions and distinctive moral characteristics."

Cardinal Newman spoke of this conflict as yet to come. Doubtless its climax is yet to come, but in essence the conflict has been going on for 2,000 years. It has not been limited to one nation or to one form of government. The issues, the slogans, the battle flags, the battlefields and the personalities have been different. But basically it has been the same encounter of opposing principles, a struggle more comprehensive, more deeprooted and even more violent than the political and military battles which go on today. It is easy to envision the struggle as being wholly physical - of men and arms - of stockpiles, strategic materials and nuclear weapons - of air bases and bombers, of industrial potential and military achievements. This is the material struggle, and the central problem here is to be equal to the sacrifices necessary for ultimate survival and victory. But of far deeper significance is "the stern encounter", the very nearly silent struggle, with no din to be heard in the streets of the world, and with weapons far more subtle and far more damaging than cannons and shells. The encounter of which I speak makes no more noise than the inner process of disintegration which over a period of several hundred years may hollow from within some great tree of the forest, until it is left standing an empty shell, the easy victim of a winter gale.

We can barely hear the stern encounter, and thus too often we forget it. Our minds, like the headlines of our newspapers, are intent upon the present and future conflicts of armed might, and upon the brutal, physical side of that ominous war upon which we have bestowed the strange epithet "cold". We tend to forget the moral and spiritual issues which inhere in the fateful encounter of which the physical war is but one manifestation. We tend to forget those ideals and faiths and philosophical needs which drive men far more intensely than military and economic objectives.

This is not to say that we have overlooked religion. Too often we have utilized it as a weapon, broadcast it as propaganda, shouted it as a battle cry. But in "the stern encounter", in the moral struggle, religion is not simply a weapon - it is the essence of the struggle itself. The Communist rulers do not fear the phraseology of religion, or the ceremonies and churches and denomination organizations. On the contrary, they leave no stone unturned in seeking to turn these aspects of religion to their own advantage and to use the trappings of religion in order to cement the obedience of their people. What they fear is the profound consequences of a religion that is lived and not merely acknowledged. They fear especially man's response to spiritual and ethical stimuli, not merely material. A society which seeks to make the worship of the State the ultimate objective of life cannot permit a higher loyalty, a faith in God, a belief in a religion that elevates the individual, acknowledges his true value and teaches him devotion and responsibility to something beyond the here and the now. The communists fear Christianity more as a way of life than as a weapon. In short, there is room in a totalitarian system for churches - but there is no room for God. The claim of the State must be total, and no other loyalty, and no other philosophy of life can be tolerated.

Is this not simply an indication of the weakness of the communist position? If the ultimate struggle is indeed a moral encounter, then are we not certain of eventual victory?

At first glance it might seem inevitable that in a struggle where the issue is the supremacy of the moral order, we must be victorious. That it is not inevitable, is due to the steady attrition in our faith and belief, a disease from which we in the West are suffering heavily. The communists have substituted dialectical materialism for faith in God; we on our part have substituted too often cynicism, indifference and secularism. We have permitted the communists too often to choose the ground for the struggle. We point with pride to the great outpourings of our factories and assume we have therefore proved the superiority of our system. We forget that the essence of the struggle is not material, but spiritual and ethical. We forget that the purpose of life is the future and not the present.

This emphasis on the material shows itself in many elements of our political life. Too often, in our foreign policy, in order to compete with the power doctrines of the Bolcheviks, we ourselves practice what Jacques Maritain called "moderate machiavellianism". But as Maritain pointed out in the showdown, this pale and attenuated version "is inevitably destined to be vanquished by absolute and virulent machiavellianism" as practiced by the communists.

We cannot separate our lives into compartments, either as individuals or as a nation. We cannot, on the one hand, run with the tide, and on the other, hold fast to Catholic principles.

Here at Assumption we are taught that Christianity is a way of life, not a means to an end: that eternal truths and the problems of this world cannot be kept separate. You who are graduating from this College today know this to be true and it is your responsibility as well as your opportunity by your works and example to stimulate a revival of our religious faith, to renew the battle against weary indifference and inertia, against the washing away of our religious, ethical and cultural foundations.

If our nation recognizes the spiritual and moral element of the "stern encounter", and directs our policies to emphasize this phase of the struggle - if we refuse those compromises which have cost us so heavily - which have blurred the nature of the encounter between our enemies and ourselves - we shall find our way easier, our success more certain.

As graduates of this College during the years of its greatest crisis, when the struggle for survival seemed crushing, you have found a clear example of what charity, hope and faith, especially faith, can do in overcoming all obstacles. The cause for which we struggle needs reaffirmation. Its true meaning and significance can be found at Assumption, and you who have studied here can be the vanguard in giving direction and purpose to our lives and to our time.

United States Military Power Speech

August 14, 1958

U.S. Senate, Washington, D.C.

Mr. President, 400 years ago the British crown and people realized with a sense of shock that they had lost Calais forever. Long considered an impregnable symbol of British supremacy in Europe, this last foothold of English power on the Continent was surrendered to the French in 1558. It is said that when Mary of England died, in the same year, the word "Calais" was engraved upon her heart - but that she was, in the words of The Cambridge Modern History, an eminent example "of the inadequacy of deep convictions and pious motives to guide the state aright." Once they had recovered from their initial panic, the British set about adjusting their thinking and their policies to the loss they had suffered. With their gateway to the Continent gone, they sought new power and influence in the seas. A navy was built, new trade routes promoted, a new maritime emphasis established; and when the Spanish Armada was defeated in 1588, the panic and pessimism that had followed the loss of Calais were forgotten as Brittania ruled the waves. The old power, the foundation for old policies, was gone - but new policies had brought a new power and new security.

The time has come for the United States to consider a similar change, if we, too, are to depend on something more than deep convictions and pious motives to guide the state aright. For we, too, are about to lose the power foundation that has long stood behind our basic military and diplomatic strategy.

THE DETERRENT RATIO

That foundation - one of the key premises upon which our leaders of diplomacy, defense, and public opinion have based their policy thinking - has been, since Hiroshima, our nuclear power. We have possessed a capacity for retaliation so great as to deter any potential aggressor from launching a direct attack upon us. Spokesmen for both parties, in the Senate and elsewhere, have debated our preparedness upon the assumption that this "ultimate deterrent" would deter any Soviet attack. Our retaliatory power, said the President in his 1958 state of the Union message, is "the most powerful deterrent to war in the world today," offering any potential aggressor "the prospect of virtual annihilation of his own country." Possession of similar striking power by the Soviet Union has not altered this basic premise - it is instead described now as the result of a "nuclear stalemate," a point of mutual "saturation" or a "balance of terror."

The hard facts of the matter are that this premise will soon no longer be correct. We are rapidly approaching that dangerous period which General Gavin and others have called the "gap" or the "missile-lag period" - a period, in the words of General Gavin, "in which our own offensive and defensive missile capabilities will lag so far behind those of the Soviets as to place us in a position of great peril."

The most critical years of the gap would appear to be 1960-1964.

This is not to say that during that period we will not retain a nuclear capacity sufficient to rain "virtual annihilation" upon the U.S.S.R. But in view of our unwillingness and inability to strike the first blow, the successful use of that capacity - and the prospects for success must be overwhelming to deter a Russian attack - actually depends upon the proper balance of six factors:

(a) The striking power of the Soviet Union that could be brought to bear upon our retaliatory power in a surprise attack. In the years of the gap this will rest primarily upon their missiles - IRBM's and ICBM's.

(b) The adequacy of American defenses to reduce the success of that Soviet striking power. This will include our distant early warning system, anti-missile missiles when available and other interceptor and defense devices.

(c) The vulnerability of American retaliatory power to destruction by any Soviet weapons penetrating our defense. Exposed missile bases and planes wing-to-wing on the ground are prime examples of this factor; although in a sense it also covers our "destruction tolerance" - the amount of devastation we could endure and still fight back.

(d) The retaliatory power of the United States, its size affecting the amount of such power remaining and available after the initial Soviet attack.

(e) The adequacy of Soviet defenses to reduce the success of our retaliation.

(f) The vulnerability of the Soviet Union and its tolerance of destruction, as a measure of what the Soviets will be able and willing to do after our retaliation.

In short, what might be called the deterrent ratio - in terms of a somewhat oversimplified formula - requires that the sum of (a), (e), and (c) be no greater than the sum of (d), (b), and (f) - if we are to have a stalemate. But as the missile striking power of the Soviet Union increases and our retaliatory power lags - as the adequacy of our continental defense falls behind that of the Soviets - as we fail to reduce sufficiently the vulnerability of our attack installations and planes, as contrasted with the wide dispersal of Soviet-Red Chinese power - and uncertain as we are about the destruction tolerance of our people whose political institutions and way of life are not prepared by tradition for the devastation of battle, again unlike the Soviets - then we must realize that the deterrent ratio during 1960-64 will in all likelihood be weighted very heavily against us.

These are not easy facts to face - and once faced, their implications are not easily comprehended. But the facts must be faced - and soon. Our peril is not simply because Russian striking power during the years of the gap will have a slight edge over us in missile power - they will have several times as many: Intermediate range missiles to devastate our own country, installations, and Government; and history's largest fleet of submarines, and possibly long-range supersonic jet bombers, to follow up this advantage. If by that time their submarines are capable of launching missiles, they could destroy 85 percent of our industry, 43 of our 50 largest cities, and most of the Nation's population.

We shall have no such supply of missiles with which to retaliate - particularly after our few exposed IRBM bases in Europe and the Mediterranean are attacked. We have not yet even successfully completed a test of our Atlas or Titan ICBM's; while Russian test successes are now established.

Progress on what appears to be one of our best hopes, the Polaris, has lagged; at least, on 4 Polaris submarines authorized by Congress in addition to the 5 already under development. I understand they may even now be threatened by a possible Defense Department order. A threat to impound funds provided by Congress is contained in a letter from Secretary McElroy to the Committee on Armed Services. We shall rely to a great extent on manned bombers - bombers which face a problem of sufficient alert and sufficient dispersal to avoid decimation, particularly if current Middle East trends should curtail our base operations in that area - bombers that lack an adequate refueling system to penetrate Soviet borders without some 2 to 4 refuelings from our inadequate tanker supply.

Even then we shall encounter a Soviet air defense, and dispersal or concealment of vulnerable power, far superior to our own - a margin, according to some estimates, which the Soviets will be able to maintain at a level 2 to 4 times greater than our own. Indeed, our own DEW system and other continental defense bulwarks - many of which the Soviets will hope to knock out before or during the first blow - were planned for manned bombers, and must be redesigned and rebuilt before they are adequate for the missile age.

In short, the deterrent ratio might well shift to the Soviets so heavily, during the years of the gap, as to open to them a new shortcut to world domination. A portion of their homeland would still almost inevitably be destroyed, no matter how great their defenses or how decimated our retaliatory power. And without doubt world opinion would not tolerate such an attack. But our experience with the illogical decisions of Adolf Hitler should have taught us that these considerations might not deter the leaders of a totalitarian state - particularly in a moment of recklessness, panic, irrationality, or even cool miscalculation.

Surely we realize that the possibilities of serious miscalculation of war by inadvertence, of having both sides caught in a course which would lead to an all-out war which neither originally contemplated, of the calling of a bluff, or of the sudden spreading of a limited war, are very real possibilities, if we but recall the Soviet Union's miscalculations on Korea in 1950, our own miscalculation of the Red Chinese reaction in 1951, our near intervention at Dienbienphu in 1954, the Soviet threats of rocket war at the time of the Suez invasion in 1956, and the possibilities of massive intervention by both sides which the situation in Iraq would have posed this year, had that struggle continued for very long. For many years, now, we have been living on the edge of the crater. We know full well the lack of communications between ourselves and our adversaries, the mutual suspicion and hostility, the increased risks taken by the Soviets as their striking power grows. Let no one think, therefore, that a Soviet attack, inadvertent or otherwise, is impossible, because of the H-bomb damage which we would still hope to rain upon the Soviets.

The Soviets, moreover, will be as well aware as we of their advantage during the years of the gap. We cannot expect them to sit idly by, and make no profitable use of it, while we strive to catch up. If General Gavin is correct in estimating Russian lead time to be twice as short as ours - 5 years, as compared to 10 - we may not even catch up in 1964, or thereafter. We cannot expect them to give us the same advantage - by sitting by until our missile power equals their own - that we gave to them during the years of our atomic monopoly.

THE NON-NUCLEAR THREAT

But nuclear destruction is not the only way in which the Soviets will be able to use their advantages in striking power. War is not so much an objective of foreign policy, as an instrument - a means of securing power and influence, of advancing a nation's views and interests. In the years of the gap, the Soviets may be expected to use their superior striking ability to achieve their objectives in ways which may not require launching an actual attack. Their missile power will be by the shield from behind which they will slowly, but surely, advance - through sputnik diplomacy, limited brushfire wars, indirect non-overt aggression, intimidation and subversion, internal revolution, increased prestige or influence, and the vicious blackmail of our allies. The periphery of the free world will slowly be nibbled away. The balance of power will gradually shift against us. The key areas vital to our security will gradually undergo Soviet infiltration and domination. Each such Soviet move will weaken the West; but none will seem sufficiently significant by itself to justify our initiating a nuclear war which might destroy us.

Throughout the years of the gap, a direct Soviet attack may be our greatest danger. But it is these other avenues of Soviet advance - with a thrust more difficult to interpret and oppose, yet inevitably ending in our isolation, submission, or destruction - which may well constitute the most likely threat.

Four hundred years ago, the English lost Calais. That event altered the course of British diplomacy and military policy, and changed the direction of British public opinion. The acceptance of the loss, and the adjustment of policy, were not easily or quickly accomplished; but they occurred eventually.

There is every indication that by 1960 the United States will have lost its Calais - its superiority in nuclear striking power. If we act now to prepare for that loss, and if, during the years of the gap, we act with both courage and prudence, there is no reason why we, too, cannot successfully emerge from this period of peril more secure than ever.

THE NEED FOR A NEW APPROACH

Unfortunately, our past reliance upon massive retaliation has stultified the development of new policy. We have developed what Henry Kissinger has called a Maginot-line mentality - dependence upon a strategy which may collapse or may never be used, but which meanwhile prevents the consideration of any alternative. When that prop is gone, the alternative seems to many to be inaction and acceptance of the inevitability of defeat. After all, once the Soviets have the power to destroy us, we have no way of absolutely preventing them from doing so. But every nation, whatever its status, needs a strategy. Some courses of action are always preferable to others; and there are alternatives to all-out war or inaction.

But the adjustment is made more difficult by our traditional failure to link our national strategy and our thinking to our military status. We have extended our commitments around the world, without regard to the sufficiency of our military posture to fulfill those commitments. Changes in our defense status are rarely reflected in our diplomatic policies, pronouncements, and planning. The State and Defense Departments negotiate with each other at arm's length, like so many Venetian envoys, without decisive leadership to break through the excess of bureaucratic committees, competition, and complacency. We think of diplomacy and force as alternatives to each other - the one to be used where the other fails - as though such absolute distinctions were still possible.

Today, we are approaching the years of the gap as though the situation were normal, and as though other assumptions were unchanged - or, in some quarters, at least, as though the problem were one of arms, alone. Nothing could be farther from the truth.

In the years of the gap, our threats of massive retaliation will lose most of their impact.

In the years of the gap, every basic assumption held by the American public with regard to our military and foreign policies will be called into question. Among the assumptions to be invalidated will be the following 10, which probably are most fundamental to our thinking in the 20th century.

First. American arms and science are superior to any others in the world.

Second. American efforts for worldwide disarmament are a selfless sacrifice for peace.

Third. Our bargaining power at any international conference table is always more vast and flexible than that of our enemy.

Fourth. Peace is a normal relation among states; and aggression is the exception - direct and unambiguous.

Fifth. We should enter every military conflict as a moral crusade requiring the unconditional surrender of the enemy.

Sixth. A free and peace-loving nation has nothing to fear in a world where right and justice inevitably prevail.

Seventh. Americans live far behind the lines, protected by time, space, and a host of allies from attack.

Eighth. We shall have time to mobilize our superior economic resources after a war begins.

Ninth. Our advanced weapons and continental defense systems, established at a tremendous cost and effort, will protect us.

Tenth. Victory ultimately goes to the nation with the highest national income, gross national product, and standard of living.

All of these concepts will be altered or questioned in but a few years. It is unthinkable that we approach the years of the gap with the same sense of normalcy, the same slogans and economies, the same assumptions, tactics, and diplomatic strategy.

Although other peoples have learned to live for years exposed to enemy attack, I realize that it is hard for us to accept the reality of our danger - particularly when we have been told each year that our defenses were daily stronger and superior to any other. I realize that we are reluctant to reexamine policies arduously reached, or to believe that these problems cannot be postponed. But it is precisely this substitution of our preferences for our responsibilities that has led us to the brink of the gap. Our missile lag is not the cause of the gap - it is but another symptom of our national complacency, our willingness to confuse the facts as they were with what we hoped they would be, to appeal at the same time to those who wanted a quick solution and those who wanted a less burdensome one. The people have been misled; the congress has been misled; and some say with good reason that on occasion the President himself has been misinformed and thus misled. For we have been passing through a period aptly described by Stanley Baldwin, in a great House of Commons debate, in disclosing Britain's unpreparedness to the House of Commons in 1936, as "the years the locusts have eaten."

THE EXAGGERATION OF ECONOMY

Perhaps the most serious result of this complacency - and the one we must first reverse - was our willingness to place fiscal security ahead of national security. We tailored our strategy and military requirements to fit our budget - instead of fitting our budget to our military requirements and strategy. We facilitated the adoption of this popular course through a variety of appealing shibboleths proclaimed to the Nation each year by the President:

Maximum safety at minimum cost (1953 state of the Union).

Sustained military capability at the lowest possible cost (1954 budget message).

Our defenses have been reinforced at sharply reduced costs (1956 state of the Union).

We cannot afford to build military strength by sacrificing economic strength (1954 budget message).

Future defense costs must be held to tolerable levels (1957 budget message).

Adequate military strength within the limits of endurable strain upon our economy (1953 state of the Union).

In recent years we have heard a good deal about an alleged quotation from Lenin who is supposed to have stated that the destruction of the capitalistic world would come about as a result of overspending on arms. I would say that has probably been the most valuable quotation the Communists have had other than "Workers of the World, Unite." But the fact of the matter is that was not said by Lenin. However, this slogan, which has been spread before us during this decade, has caused us constantly to emphasize economic considerations rather than military considerations, and has been used as an authority for that policy. The fact is that Lenin never stated it. Nevertheless, I should think that in the future it would rank high among the slogans which had proved to be useful in the effort to destroy the capitalistic system.

There were many others. The rationale was simple:

To build excessively * * * could defeat our purposes and impair or destroy the very freedom and economic system our military defenses are designed to protect (1956). * * * Any program that endangers our economy could defeat us (1957). * * * To amass military power without regard to our economic capacity would be to defend ourselves against one kind of disaster by inviting another (1953).

The fact of the matter is that during that period when emphasis was laid upon our economic strength instead of our military strength, we were losing the decisive years when we could have maintained a lead against the Soviet Union in our missile capacity. These were the vital years we lost, the years the locusts have eaten, and it is quite obvious we obtained economic security at the expense of military security, and that this policy will bring us into great danger within the next few years.

I have never been very persuaded by this argument. It has always seemed to me that the converse was much more persuasive - that to emphasize budgetary limitations without regard to our military position was to avoid an inconvenient effort by inviting the disaster that would destroy all budgets and conveniences. Surely our Nation's security overrides budgetary considerations - the President himself indicated this was true in times of war. Then why can we not realize that the coming years of the gap present us with a peril more deadly than any wartime danger we have ever known? And most important of all - and most tragically ironic - our Nation could have afforded, and can afford now, the steps necessary to close the missile gap.

But our task now is not to fix the blame for the past, but to fix a course for the future.

NEW MILITARY STEPS

Our attention is logically and necessarily directed first at the short-range military steps necessary to keep the deterrent ratio from shifting still further to the Red side and to lessen their advantage, if possible. Here other Senators have distinguished themselves in thoughtful addresses or committee action - including in particular the majority leader, Mr. Johnson, the junior Senator from Missouri, Mr. Symington, and the junior Senator from Washington, Mr. Jackson.

More air tankers to refuel our SAC bombers and more air-to-ground missiles to lessen the need for their deep penetration of Soviet territory are among the first steps to be taken while we expedite our longer range ICBM and IRBM developments, and our progress on atomic submarines, solid fuels, the Polaris, and the Minuteman. Our continental defense system, as already mentioned, must be redesigned for the detection and interception of missile attacks as well as planes.

It should be obvious from our Lebanon experience that we lack the sea and air-lift necessary to intervene in a limited war with the speed, discrimination, and versatility which may well be needed to keep it limited - and without weakening our ultimate retaliatory power. It is shocking to realize that units entering the Lebanon pipeline at the time of the Iraqi revolt emerged at the other end to find that by then the dust had settled and we had already recognized the new regime and it was time to evacuate.

We need to reduce what General Gavin describes as a "critical cut" in our military manpower begun in 1954. With the support of a majority on this side of the aisle, I offered an amendment in 1954 to block a cut in military divisions from 19 to 17; but as General Gavin now points out:

Congress was assured that our combat strength was not being reduced. We were simply cutting the fat * * * That the contrary was the case few outside the Department of the Army seemed willing to admit.

Finally, if we do not take care, we will create a second gap - between the date when our present ready weapons are obsolescent and the date when our ballistic missiles are operational in any sufficient quantity. To prevent this short-term gap, and to make certain that we have ended the missile-lag by 1964, when we shall have mass production, we hope, of the Minuteman solid-fuel missile, may well require a complete reexamination of our traditional systems of evaluating, budgeting, researching, assigning, developing, and procuring weapons.

NEW STRATEGIC POLICIES

But discussions of new armaments are not enough - and too late to halt the gap. The gap will begin in 1960. And while stepped-up defense efforts are essential to insure its close in 1964 and thereafter, and to lessen its impact in between, the years of the gap demand something more than a purely military answer.

A Maginot-line reliance upon the military answer of massive retaliation has frustrated policy discussions to date, as mentioned - we must now be prepared to demonstrate that we have other courses besides military action and no action at all. For absence of power no more dictates an absence of policy than the presence of power. On the contrary, ancient man survived the more powerful beasts about him because his wisdom - his strategy and his policies - overcame his lack of power. We can do the same. We dare not attempt less, nor do we dare rely wholly upon those same policies in effect during the years of our retaliatory lead.

What is the fundamental approach to formulating a strategy from a basically but only temporarily disadvantageous position? It is first, of necessity, to work for a real peace - for a reduction of armaments, a reduction of tensions, and a reduction of areas of dispute. The goal of universal disarmament - at least in the area of nuclear weapons and long range ballistic missiles - takes on an urgency not heretofore demonstrated by American negotiators who felt they held most of the trump cards. We must redouble our efforts in that regard - and the work of the Senate Disarmament Subcommittee, headed by the distinguished junior Senator from Minnesota, Mr. Humphrey, has made a major contribution to illuminating areas where our efforts might be redoubled.

But that failing, as well it might, once the Soviets are in the driver's seat, though we must never stop trying - the question again arises as to what basic strategy we employ during the years of the gap.

The best and most recent example is that provided by the Soviets themselves during the years of their gap - when American might was superior. While we would not imitate the Communists per se, they demonstrated the classic strategy of the underdog - and soon we will be the underdog. It is basically a strategy of making the most of all remaining advantages and making the most of the enemy's weaknesses - and for us to buy the time and opportunity necessary to regain the upper hand. This will require not only strong leadership in Washington but also expert ambassadors in the field - men equal to the best of any other nation, who are skilled in the needed techniques of probe and prudence, and whose judgments and reports are more reliable than some of those which misled us in Indochina and other difficult areas in years gone by.

Twentieth Century America is not accustomed to this underdog strategy - although it was expertly practiced by our Founding Fathers in time of peace as well as war. And we can practice it now.

Consider for a moment the advantages we retain even after our retaliatory lead is lost:

We retain an economic and industrial advantage, of little use once a bomb is dropped, but of considerable use now in building situations of strength and goodwill in such key areas as India and Tunisia. There is no need to waste this advantage in a drawn-out recession - and the Congress has an important opportunity to utilize this advantage in an action this week on the Development Loan Fund - the best hope for nations seeking the capital necessary to outstrip their population increases.

We retain an ideological advantage, better equipped than any nation in the world to export the revolutionary ideas of the Declaration of Independence, and thus lead, not frustrate, the nationalist movement against imperialism of any variety, East and West. Particularly after our recent excursion in the Middle East, we are regarded in too many parts of the world as an enemy of popular rule - when we had every right to enjoy the cleanest, strongest reputation in this regard of any nation on earth.

We retain a geographical advantage, essential to adequate dispersal and warning systems, and to the encouragement of local resistance to the Red tide. Although, as Mr. Dulles has said, we cannot make popularity our goal, we must shape our attitudes and procedures in a way that will not cost us our geographical advantage. We do not retain that advantage simply through paper alliances with the reactionary, unpopular governments which have no indigenous support; and recent events in the Middle East should also have taught us that, to maintain that geographical advantage, no commitment at all is better than one which we cannot or should not honor, which the local populations did not request, which our allies do not support, and which is politically or militarily unfeasible.

How well we learned that lesson, to be more precise and to compare strength, may soon be tested in the case of Quemoy and Matsu. I do not think there is greater folly than to leave our commitment in that area as vague as the Secretary of State has left it. If the Chinese should assume we are not going to come to the defense of Quemoy and Matsu, and it is the intention of the United states to come to the aid of those islands, we could find ourselves embroiled in a struggle which could lead to a major political action and perhaps to disaster for all of us, East and West.

As we approach the years of the gap, the U.S.S.R. will also retain weaknesses for us to probe - chief among them is the Achilles heel of the satellite nations. The Congress and administration must reverse those policies, last affirmed by a 1-vote margin in June, which hamstring our flexibility in attempting to wean the satellites from the Soviets, and to drive new wedges into each new crack in the Iron Curtain.

It is interesting, at a time when we are being charged before the United Nations with carrying on an imperialistic policy in the Middle East, to note that the Soviet Union should have begun to tighten in the most formidable way the screws of its control in Poland by an attempt to crack down and destroy the independence of the church, which is the largest single force within Poland against the

Stalinist policies of some of the Communist leaders. That is the most genuine imperialism. It is to be hoped United States policies will be clear throughout the world to exploit it and to spotlight it, in our own efforts, in our own propaganda, and in our own diplomacy.

There is no point now in consolidating the Red bloc with our talk of massive retaliation - now we must seek ways of dividing it.

In short, to sound the alarm is not to panic - it is not to sell America short. It gives the enemy no encouragement he did not already possess. But the sound of the alarm does warn us that time is running out - that no matter how complex the problems, how discouraging the prospects, or how unpopular the decisions, these facts must be faced. Complacency or hysteria will not help. Sustained and informed constructive effort will help - not to provide all the answers for the future, but to help assure us that there will be a future.

In Gibbon's volumes on the Decline and Fall of the Roman Empire he stated that the Romans maintained the peace by a constant preparation for war and that they indicated to the enemies on their periphery they were as little disposed to endure injury as to offer it. I do not say we should only prepare for war. But we should certainly use all elements of national policy - economic, diplomatic, and military - in order to prepare us for the most serious test in our Nation's history, which will be impending in the next 5 years.

No Pearl Harbor, no Dunkirk, no Calais is sufficient to end us permanently if we but find the will and the way.

In the words of Sir Winston Churchill in a dark time of England's history:

Come then - let us to the task, to the battle and the toil - each to our part, each to our station * * * Let us go forward together in all parts of the (land). There is not a week, nor a day, nor an hour to be lost.

The Presidency in 1960 Speech

January 14, 1960
National Press Club, Washington, D.C.

The modern presidential campaign covers every issue in and out of the platform from cranberries to creation. But the public is rarely alerted to a candidate's views about the central issue on which all the rest turn. That central issue--and the point of my comments this noon-- is not the farm problem or defense or India. It is the presidency itself.

Of course a candidate's views on specific policies are important, but Theodore Roosevelt and William Howard Taft shared policy views with entirely different results in the White House. Of course it is important to elect a good man with good intentions, but Woodrow Wilson and Warren G. Harding were both good men with good intentions; so were Lincoln and Buchanan; but there is a Lincoln Room in the White House and no Buchanan Room.

The history of this Nation--its brightest and its bleakest pages-- has been written largely in terms of the different views our Presidents have had of the Presidency itself. This history ought to tell us that the American people in 1960 have an imperative right to know what any man bidding for the Presidency thinks about the place he is bidding for, whether he is aware of and willing to use the powerful resources of that office; whether his model will be Taft or Roosevelt, Wilson or Harding.

Not since the days of Woodrow Wilson has any candidate spoken on the presidency itself before the votes have been irrevocably cast. Let us hope that the 1960 campaign, in addition to discussing the familiar issues where our positions too often blur, will also talk about the presidency itself, as an instrument for dealing with those issues, as an office with varying roles, powers, and limitations

During the past 8 years, we have seen one concept of the Presidency at work. Our needs and hopes have been eloquently stated--but the initiative and follow-through have too often been left to others. And too often his own objectives have been lost by the President's failure to override objections from within his own party, in the Congress or even in his Cabinet.

The American people in 1952 and 1956 may have preferred this detached, limited concept of the Presidency after 20 years of fast-moving, creative Presidential rule. Perhaps historians will regard this as necessarily one of those frequent periods of consolidation, a time to draw breath, to recoup our national energy. To quote the state of the Union message: "No Congress . . . on surveying the state of the Nation, has met with a more pleasing prospect than that which appears at the present time."

Unfortunately this is not Mr. Eisenhower's last message to the Congress, but Calvin Coolidge's. He followed to the White House Mr. Harding, whose sponsor declared very frankly that the times did not demand a first-rate President. If true, the times and the man met.

But the question is what do the times--and the people--demand for the next 4 years in the White House?

They demand a vigorous proponent of the national interest--not a passive broker for conflicting private interests. They demand a man capable of acting as the commander in chief of the Great Alliance, not merely a bookkeeper who feels that his work is done when the numbers on the balance sheet come even. They demand that he be the head of a responsible party, not rise so far above politics as to be invisible--a man who will formulate and fight for legislative policies, not be a casual bystander to the legislative process.

Today a restricted concept of the Presidency is not enough. For beneath today's surface gloss of peace and prosperity are increasingly dangerous, unsolved, long postponed problems--problems that will inevitably explode to the surface during the next

4 years of the next administration--the growing missile gap, the rise of Communist China, the despair of the underdeveloped nations, the explosive situations in Berlin and in the Formosa Straits, the deterioration of NATO, the lack of an arms control agreement, and all the domestic problems of our farms, cities, and schools.

This administration has not faced up to these and other problems. Much has been said--but I am reminded of the old Chinese proverb: "There is a great deal of noise on the stairs but nobody comes into the room."

The President's state of the Union message reminded me of the exhortation from "King Lear" but goes: "I will do such things--what they are I know not . . . but they shall be the wonders of the earth."

In the decade that lies ahead--in the challenging revolutionary sixties--the American Presidency will demand more than ringing manifestoes issued from the rear of the battle. It will demand that the President place himself in the very thick of the fight, that he care passionately about the fate of the people he leads, that he be willing to serve them, at the risk of incurring their momentary displeasure.

Whatever the political affiliation of our next President, whatever his views may be on all the issues and problems that rush in upon us, he must above all be the Chief Executive in every sense of the word. He must be prepared to exercise the fullest powers of his office--all that are specified and some that are not. He must master complex problems as well as receive one-page memorandums. He must originate action as well as study groups. He must reopen channels of communication between the world of thought and the seat of power.

Ulysses Grant considered the President "a purely administrative officer." If he administered the overnment departments efficiently, delegated his functions smoothly, and performed his ceremonies of state with decorum and grace, no more was to be expected of him. But that is not the place the Presidency was meant to have in

American life. The President is alone, at the top--the loneliest job there is, as Harry Truman has said.

If there is destructive dissension among the services, he alone can step in and straighten it out--instead of waiting for unanimity. If administrative agencies are not carrying out their mandate--if a brushfire threatens some part of the globe--he alone can act, without waiting for the Congress. If his farm program fails, he alone deserves the blame, not his Secretary of Agriculture.

"The President is at liberty, both in law and conscience, to be as big a man as he can." So wrote Prof. Woodrow Wilson. But President Woodrow Wilson discovered that to be a big man in the White House inevitably brings cries of dictatorship.

So did Lincoln and Jackson and the two Roosevelts. And so may the next occupant of that office, if he is the man the times demand. But how much better it would be, in the turbulent sixties, to have a Roosevelt or a Wilson than to have another James Buchanan, cringing in the White House, afraid to move.

Nor can we afford a Chief Executive who is praised primarily for what he did not do, the disasters he prevented, the bills he vetoed-- a President wishing his subordinates would produce more missiles or build more schools. We will need instead what the Constitution envisioned: a Chief Executive who is the vital center of action in our whole scheme of Government.

This includes the legislative process as well. The President cannot afford--for the sake of the office as well as the Nation--to be another Warren G. Harding, described by one backer as a man who "would when elected, sign whatever bill the Senate sent him--and not send bills for the Senate to pass." Rather he must know when to lead the Congress when to consult it and when he should act alone.

Having served 14 years in the legislative branch, I would not look with favor upon its domination by the Executive. Under our government of "power as the rival of power," to use Hamilton's phrase, Congress must not surrender its responsibilities. But neither should it dominate. However large its share in the formulation of domestic programs, it is the President alone who must make the major decisions of our foreign policy.

That is what the Constitution wisely commands. And even domestically, the President must initiate policies and devise laws to meet the needs of the Nation. And he must be prepared to use all the resources of his office to ensure the enactment of that legislation--even when conflict is the result.

By the end of his term Theodore Roosevelt was not popular in the Congress--particularly when he criticized an amendment to the Treasury appropriation which forbade the use of Secret Service men to investigate Congressmen.

And the feeling was mutual, Roosevelt saying: "I do not much admire the Senate because it is such a helpless body when efficient work is to be done."

And Woodrow Wilson was even more bitter after his frustrating quarrels. Asked if he might run for the Senate in 1920, he replied: "Outside of the United States, the Senate does not amount to a damn. And inside the United States the Senate is mostly despised. They haven't had a thought down there in 50 years."

But, however bitter their farewells, the facts of the matter are that Roosevelt and Wilson did get things done--not only through their Executive powers but through the Congress as well. Calvin Coolidge, on the other hand, departed from Washington with cheers of Congress still ringing in his ears. But when his World Court bill was under fire on Capitol Hill he sent no message, gave no encouragement to the bill's leaders, and paid little or no attention to the whole proceeding--and the cause of world justice was set back.

To be sure, Coolidge had held the usual White House breakfasts with congressional leaders--but they were aimed, as he himself said, at "good fellowship," not a discussion of "public business." And at his press conferences, according to press historians, where he preferred to talk about the local flower show and its exhibits, reporters who finally extracted from him a single sentence--"I'm against that bill"--would rush to file tongue-in-cheek dispatches claiming that: "President Coolidge, in a fighting mood, today served notice on Congress that he intended to combat, with all the resources at his command, the pending bill . . ."

But in the coming months we will need a real fighting mood in the White House--a man who will not retreat in the face of pressure from his congressional leaders--who will not let down those supporting his views on the floor. Divided Government over the past 6 years has only been further confused by this lack of legislative leadership. To restore it next year will help restore purpose to both the Presidency and the Congress.

The facts of the matter are that legislative leadership is not possible without party leadership, in the most political sense--and Mr. Eisenhower prefers to stay above politics (although a weekly news magazine last fall reported the startling news, and I quote, that "President Eisenhower is emerging as a major political figure"). When asked early in his first term, how he liked the "game of politics," he replied with a frown that his questioner was using a derogatory phrase. "Being President," he said, "is a very great experience . . . but the word 'politics' . . . I have no great liking for that."

But no President, it seems to me, can escape politics. He has not only been chosen by the Nation--he has been chosen by his party. And if he insists that he is "President of all the people" and should, therefore, offend none of them--if he blurs the issues and differences between the parties--if he neglects the party machinery and avoids his party's leadership--then he has not only weakened the political party as an instrument of the democratic process--he has dealt a blow to the democratic process itself.

I prefer the example of Abe Lincoln, who loved politics with the passion of a born practitioner. For example, he waited up all night in 1863 to get the crucial returns on the Ohio governorship. When the Unionist candidate was elected, Lincoln wired: "Glory God in the highest. Ohio has saved the Nation."

But the White House is not only the center of political leadership. It must be the center of moral leadership--a "bully pulpit," as Theodore Roosevelt described it. For only the President represents the national interest. And upon him alone converge all the needs and aspirations of all parts of the country, all departments of the Government, all nations of the world.

It is not enough merely to represent prevailing sentiment--to follow McKinley's practice, as described by Joe Cannon, of "keeping his ear so close to the ground he got it full of grasshoppers." We will need in the sixties a President who is willing and able to summon his national constituency to its finest hour--to alert the people to our dangers and our opportunities--to demand of them the sacrifices that will be necessary. Despite the increasing evidence of a lost national purpose and a soft national will, F.D.R.'s words in his first inaugural still ring true: "In every dark hour of our national life, a leadership of frankness and vigor has met with that understanding and support of the people themselves which is essential to victory."

Roosevelt fulfilled the role of moral leadership. So did Wilson and Lincoln, Truman and Jackson and Teddy Roosevelt. They led the people as well as the Government--they fought for great ideals as well as bills. And the time has come to demand that kind of leadership again.

And so, as this vital campaign begins, let us discuss the issues the next President will face--but let us also discuss the powers and tools with which we must face them.

For we must endow that office with extraordinary strength and vision. We must act in the image of Abraham Lincoln summoning his wartime Cabinet to a meeting on the Emancipation

Proclamation. That Cabinet has [sic] been carefully chosen to please and reflect many elements in the country. But "I have gathered you together," Lincoln said, "to hear what I have written down. I do not wish your advice about the main matter--that I have determined for myself."

And later, when he went to sign, after several hours of exhausting handshaking that had left his arm weak, he said to those present: "If my name goes down in history, it will be for this act. My whole soul is in it. If my hand trembles when I sign this proclamation, all who examine the document hereafter will say: 'He hesitated.'"

But Lincoln's hand did not tremble. He did not hesitate. He did not equivocate. For he was the President of the United States.

It is in this spirit that we must go forth in the coming months and years.

The President-Elect's Address

January 9, 1961

The State House, Boston, Massachusetts

I have welcomed this opportunity to address this historic body, and, through you, the people of Massachusetts to whom I am so deeply indebted for a lifetime of friendship and trust.

For fourteen years I have placed my confidence in the citizens of Massachusetts--and they have generously responded by placing their confidence in me.

Now, on the Friday after next, I am to assume new and broader responsibilities. But I am not here to bid farewell to Massachusetts.

For forty-three years--whether I was in London, Washington, the South Pacific, or elsewhere--this has been my home; and, God willing, wherever I serve this shall remain my home.

It was here my grandparents were born--it is here I hope my grandchildren will be born.

I speak neither from false provincial pride nor artful political flattery. For no man about to enter high office in this country can ever be unmindful of the contribution this state has made to our national greatness.

Its leaders have shaped our destiny long before the great republic was born. Its principles have guided our footsteps in times of crisis as well as in times of calm. Its democratic institutions--including this historic body--have served as beacon lights for other nations as well as our sister states.

For what Pericles said to the Athenians has long been true of this commonwealth: "We do not imitate--for we are a model to others."

And so it is that I carry with me from this state to that high and lonely office to which I now succeed more than fond memories of firm friendships. The enduring qualities of Massachusetts--the common threads woven by the Pilgrim and the Puritan, the fisherman and the farmer, the Yankee and the immigrant--will not be and could not be forgotten in this nation's executive mansion.

They are an indelible part of my life, my convictions, my view of the past, and my hopes for the future.

Allow me to illustrate: During the last sixty days, I have been at the task of constructing an administration. It has been a long and deliberate process. Some have counseled greater speed. Others have counseled more expedient tests.

But I have been guided by the standard John Winthrop set before his shipmates on the flagship *Arbella* three hundred and thirty-one years ago, as they, too, faced the task of building a new government on a perilous frontier.

"We must always consider," he said, "that we shall be as a city upon a hill--the eyes of all people are upon us."

Today the eyes of all people are truly upon us--and our governments, in every branch, at every level, national, state and local, must be as a city upon a hill--constructed and inhabited by men aware of their great trust and their great responsibilities.

For we are setting out upon a voyage in 1961 no less hazardous than that undertaken by the Arabella in 1630. We are committing ourselves to tasks of statecraft no less awesome than that of governing the Massachusetts Bay Colony, beset as it was then by terror without and disorder within.

History will not judge our endeavors--and a government cannot be selected--merely on the basis of color or creed or even party affiliation. Neither will competence and loyalty and stature, while essential to the utmost, suffice in times such as these.

For of those to whom much is given, much is required. And when at some future date the high court of history sits in judgment on each one of us--recording whether in our brief span of service we fulfilled our responsibilities to the state--our success or failure, in whatever office we may hold, will be measured by the answers to four questions:

First, were we truly men of courage--with the courage to stand up to one's enemies--and the courage to stand up, when necessary, to one's associates--the courage to resist public pressure, as well as private greed?

Secondly, were we truly men of judgment--with perceptive judgment of the future as well as the past--of our own mistakes as well as the mistakes of others--with enough wisdom to know that we did not know, and enough candor to admit it?

Third, were we truly men of integrity--men who never ran out on either the principles in which they believed or the people who believed in them--men who believed in us--men whom neither financial gain nor political ambition could ever divert from the fulfillment of our sacred trust?

Finally, were we truly men of dedication--with an honor mortgaged to no single individual or group, and compromised by no private obligation or aim, but devoted solely to serving the public good and the national interest.

Courage--judgment--integrity--dedication--these are the historic qualities of the Bay Colony and the Bay State--the qualities which this state has consistently sent to this chamber on Beacon Hill here in Boston and to Capitol Hill back in Washington.

And these are the qualities which, with God's help, this son of Massachusetts hopes will characterize our government's conduct in the four stormy years that lie ahead.

Humbly I ask His help in that undertaking--but aware that on earth His will is worked by men. I ask for your help and your prayers, as I embark on this new and solemn journey.

The Presidency

First Inaugural Address

January 20, 1961
Washington, D.C.

Vice President Johnson, Mr. Speaker, Mr. Chief Justice, President Eisenhower, Vice president Nixon, President Truman, Reverend Clergy, fellow citizens:

We observe today not a victory of party but a celebration of freedom--symbolizing an end as well as a beginning--signifying renewal as well as change. For I have sworn before you and Almighty God the same solemn oath our forebears prescribed nearly a century and three quarters ago.

The world is very different now. For man holds in his mortal hands the power to abolish all forms of human poverty and all forms of human life. And yet the same revolutionary beliefs for which our forebears fought are still at issue around the globe-the belief that the rights of man come not from the generosity of the state but from the hand of God.

We dare not forget today that we are the heirs of that first revolution. Let the word go forth from this time and place, to friend and foe alike, that the torch has been passed to a new generation of Americans--born in this century, tempered by war, disciplined by a hard and bitter peace, proud of our ancient heritage--and unwilling to witness or permit the slow undoing of those human rights to which this nation has always been committed, and to which we are committed today at home and around the world.

Let every nation know, whether it wishes us well or ill, that we shall pay any price, bear any burden, meet any hardship, support any friend, oppose any foe to assure the survival and the success of liberty.

This much we pledge--and more.

To those old allies whose cultural and spiritual origins we share, we pledge the loyalty of faithful friends. United, there is little we cannot do in a host of cooperative ventures. Divided, there is little we can do--for we dare not meet a powerful challenge at odds and split asunder.

To those new states whom we welcome to the ranks of the free, we pledge our word that one form of colonial control shall not have passed away merely to be replaced by a far more iron tyranny. We shall not always expect to find them supporting our view. But we shall always hope to find them strongly supporting their own freedom-and to remember that, in the past, those who foolishly sought power by riding the back of the tiger ended up inside.

To those peoples in the huts and villages of half the globe struggling to break the bonds of mass misery, we pledge our best efforts to help them help themselves, for whatever period is required--not because the communists may be doing it, not because we seek their votes, but because it is right. If a free society cannot help the many who are poor, it cannot save the few who are rich.

To our sister republics south of our border, we offer a special pledge--to convert our good words into good deeds--in a new alliance for progress--to assist free men and free governments in casting off the chains of poverty. But this peaceful revolution of hope cannot become the prey of hostile powers. Let all our neighbors know that we shall join with them to oppose aggression or subversion anywhere in the Americas. And let every other power know that this Hemisphere intends to remain the master of its own house.

To that world assembly of sovereign states, the United Nations, our last best hope in an age where the instruments of war have far outpaced the instruments of peace, we renew our pledge of support--to prevent it from becoming merely a forum for invective--to strengthen its shield of the new and the weak--and to enlarge the area in which its writ may run.

Finally, to those nations who would make themselves our adversary, we offer not a pledge but a request: that both sides begin anew the quest for peace, before the dark powers of destruction unleashed by science engulf all humanity in planned or accidental self-destruction.

We dare not tempt them with weakness. For only when our arms are sufficient beyond doubt can we be certain beyond doubt that they will never be employed.

But neither can two great and powerful groups of nations take comfort from our present course--both sides overburdened by the cost of modern weapons, both rightly alarmed by the steady spread of the deadly atom, yet both racing to alter that uncertain balance of terror that stays the hand of mankind's final war.

So let us begin anew--remembering on both sides that civility is not a sign of weakness, and sincerity is always subject to proof. Let us never negotiate out of fear. But let us never fear to negotiate.

Let both sides explore what problems unite us instead of belaboring those problems which divide us.

Let both sides, for the first time, formulate serious and precise proposals for the inspection and control of arms--and bring the absolute power to destroy other nations under the absolute control of all nations.

Let both sides seek to invoke the wonders of science instead of its terrors. Together let us explore the stars, conquer the deserts, eradicate disease, tap the ocean depths and encourage the arts and commerce.

Let both sides unite to heed in all corners of the earth the command of Isaiah--to "undo the heavy burdens . . . (and) let the oppressed go free."

And if a beach-head of cooperation may push back the jungle of suspicion, let both sides join in creating a new endeavor, not a new balance of power, but a new world of law, where the strong are just and the weak secure and the peace preserved.

All this will not be finished in the first one hundred days. Nor will it be finished in the first one thousand days, nor in the life of this Administration, nor even perhaps in our lifetime on this planet. But let us begin.

In your hands, my fellow citizens, more than mine, will rest the final success or failure of our course. Since this country was founded, each generation of Americans has been summoned to give testimony to its national loyalty. The graves of young Americans who answered the call to service surround the globe.

Now the trumpet summons us again-not as a call to bear arms, though arms we need--not as a call to battle, though embattled we are--but a call to bear the burden of a long twilight struggle, year in and year out, "rejoicing in hope, patient in tribulation"--a struggle against the common enemies of man: tyranny, poverty, disease and war itself.

Can we forge against these enemies a grand and global alliance, North and South, East and West, that can assure a more fruitful life for all mankind? Will you join in that historic effort?

In the long history of the world, only a few generations have been granted the role of defending freedom in its hour of maximum danger. I do not shrink from this responsibility--I welcome it. I do not believe that any of us would exchange places with any other people or any other generation. The energy, the faith, the devotion which we bring to this endeavor will light our country and all who serve it--and the glow from that fire can truly light the world.

And so, my fellow Americans: ask not what your country can do for you--ask what you can do for your country.

My fellow citizens of the world: ask not what America will do for you, but what together we can do for the freedom of man.

Finally, whether you are citizens of America or citizens of the world, ask of us here the same high standards of strength and sacrifice which we ask of you. With a good conscience our only sure reward, with history the final judge of our deeds, let us go forth to lead the land we love, asking His blessing and His help, but knowing that here on earth God's work must truly be our own.

Address on Recent Events in Cuba

April 20, 1961

American Society of Newspaper Editors, Washington, D.C.

Mr. Catledge, members of the American Society of Newspaper Editors, ladies and gentlemen:

The President of a great democracy such as ours, and the editors of great newspapers such as yours, owe a common obligation to the people: an obligation to present the facts, to present them with candor, and to present them in perspective. It is with that obligation in mind that I have decided in the last 24 hours to discuss briefly at this time the recent events in Cuba.

On that unhappy island, as in so many other arenas of the contest for freedom, the news has grown worse instead of better. I have emphasized before that this was a struggle of Cuban patriots against a Cuban dictator. While we could not be expected to hide our sympathies, we made it repeatedly clear that the armed forces of this country would not intervene in any way.

Any unilateral American intervention, in the absence of an external attack upon ourselves or an ally, would have been contrary to our traditions and to our international obligations. But let the record show that our restraint is not inexhaustible. Should it ever appear that the inter-American doctrine of non-interference merely conceals or excuses a policy of nonaction-if the nations of this Hemisphere should fail to meet their commitments against outside Communist penetration-then I want it clearly understood that this Government will not hesitate in meeting its primary obligations which are to the security of our Nation!

Should that time ever come, we do not intend to be lectured on "intervention" by those whose character was stamped for all time on the bloody streets of Budapest! Nor would we expect or accept the same outcome which this small band of gallant Cuban refugees must have known that they were chancing, determined as they were against heavy odds to pursue their courageous attempts to regain their Island's freedom.

But Cuba is not an island unto itself; and our concern is not ended by mere expressions of nonintervention or regret. This is not the first time in either ancient or recent history that a small band of freedom fighters has engaged the armor of totalitarianism.

It is not the first time that Communist tanks have rolled over gallant men and women fighting to redeem the independence of their homeland. Nor is it by any means the final episode in the eternal struggle of liberty against tyranny, anywhere on the face of the globe, including Cuba itself.

Mr. Castro has said that these were mercenaries. According to press reports, the final message to be relayed from the refugee forces on the beach came from the rebel commander when asked if he wished to be evacuated. His answer was: "I will never leave this country." That is not the reply of a mercenary. He has gone now to join in the mountains countless other guerrilla fighters, who are equally determined that the dedication of those who gave their lives shall not be forgotten, and that Cuba must not be abandoned to the Communists. And we do not intend to abandon it either!

The Cuban people have not yet spoken their final piece. And I have no doubt that they and their Revolutionary Council, led by Dr. Cardona-and members of the families of the Revolutionary Council, I am informed by the Doctor yesterday, are involved themselves in the Islands-will continue to speak up for a free and independent Cuba.

Meanwhile we will not accept Mr. Castro's attempts to blame this nation for the hatred which his onetime supporters now regard his repression. But there are from this sobering episode useful lessons for us all to learn. Some may be still obscure, and await further information. Some are clear today.

First, it is clear that the forces of communism are not to be underestimated, in Cuba or anywhere else in the world. The advantages of a police state-its use of mass terror and arrests to prevent the spread of free dissent--cannot be overlooked by those who expect the fall of every fanatic tyrant. If the self-discipline of the free cannot match the iron discipline of the mailed fist-in economic, political, scientific and all the other kinds of struggles as well as the military-then the peril to freedom will continue to rise.

Secondly, it is clear that this Nation, in concert with all the free nations of this hemisphere, must take an ever closer and more realistic look at the menace of external Communist intervention and domination in Cuba. The American people are not complacent about Iron Curtain tanks and planes less than 90 miles from their shore. But a nation of Cuba's size is less a threat to our survival than it is a base for subverting the survival of other free nations throughout the hemisphere. It is not primarily our interest or our security but theirs which is now, today, in the greater peril. It is for their sake as well as our own that we must show our will.

The evidence is clear-and the hour is late. We and our Latin friends will have to face the fact that we cannot postpone any longer the real issue of survival of freedom in this hemisphere itself. On that issue, unlike perhaps some others, there can be no middle ground. Together we must build a hemisphere where freedom can flourish; and where any free nation under outside attack of any kind can be assured that all of our resources stand ready to respond to any request for assistance.

Third, and finally, it is clearer than ever that we face a relentless struggle in every corner of the globe that goes far beyond the clash of armies or even nuclear armaments. The armies are there, and in large number. The nuclear armaments are there. But they serve primarily as the shield behind which subversion, infiltration, and a host of other tactics steadily advance, picking off vulnerable areas one by one in situations which do not permit our own armed intervention.

Power is the hallmark of this offensive power and discipline and deceit. The legitimate discontent of yearning people is exploited. The legitimate trappings of self-determination are employed. But once in power, all talk of discontent is repressed; all self-determination disappears, and the promise of a revolution of hope is betrayed, as in Cuba, into-a reign of terror. Those who on instruction staged automatic "riots" in the streets of free nations over the efforts of a small group of young Cubans to regain their freedom should recall the long roll call of refugees who cannot now go back-to Hungary, to North Korea, to North Viet-Nam, to East Germany, or to Poland, or to any of the other lands from which a steady stream of refugees pours forth, in eloquent testimony to the cruel oppression now holding sway in their homeland.

We dare not fail to see the insidious nature of this new and deeper struggle. We dare not fail to grasp the new concepts, the new tools, the new sense of urgency we will need to combat it-whether in Cuba or South Viet-Nam. And we dare not fail to realize that this struggle is taking place every day, without fanfare, in thousands of villages and markets-day and night-and in classrooms all over the globe.

The message of Cuba, of Laos, of the rising din of Communist voices in Asia and Latin America-these messages are all the same. The complacent, the self-indulgent, the soft societies are about to be swept away with the debris of history. Only the strong, only the industrious, only the determined, only the courageous, only the visionary who determine the real nature of our struggle can possibly survive.

No greater task faces this country or this administration. No other challenge is more deserving of our every effort and energy. Too long we have fixed our eyes on traditional military needs, on armies prepared to cross borders, on missiles poised for flight. Now it should be clear that this is no longer enough-that our security may be lost piece by piece, country by country, without the bring of a single missile or the crossing of a single border.

We intend to profit from this lesson. We intend to reexamine and reorient our forces of all kinds-cur tactics and our institutions here in this community. We intend to intensify our efforts for a struggle in many ways more difficult than war, where disappointment will often accompany us.

For I am convinced that we in this country and in the free world possess the necessary resource, and the skill, and the added strength that comes from a belief in the freedom of man. And I am equally convinced that history will record the fact that this bitter struggle reached its climax in the late 1950's and the early 1960's Let me then make clear as the President of the United States that I am determined upon our system's survival and success, regardless of the cost and regardless of the peril!

PT 109 Cmdr John F. Kennedy (far right) with crew, Solomon Islands, 1943

President John F. Kennedy in Berlin, 1963

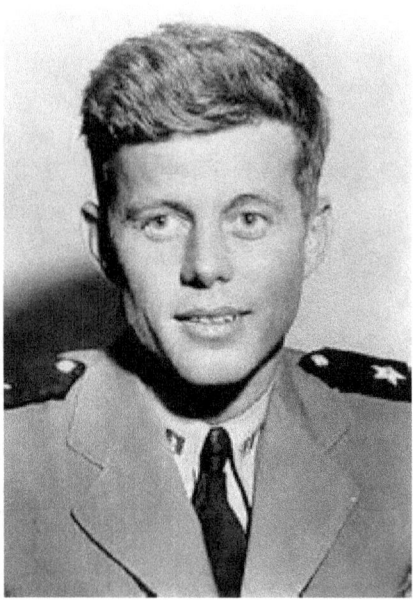

U.S. Naval Officer John F. Kennedy, 1942, during World War II

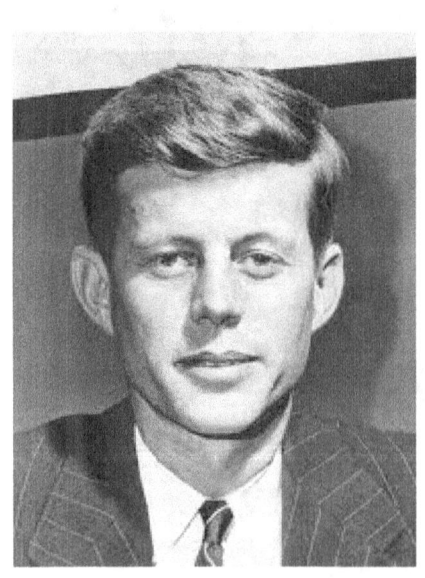

Congressman Kennedy, 1947   Senator Kennedy, 1956

Inauguration of President Kennedy, January 20, 1961

Rice University Address, 1962

Cuban Missile Crisis Address to the Nation, October 22, 1962

John F. Kennedy enjoying a Sailing, 1963

JFK using the television as a bully pulpit, 1963

President John F. Kennedy's Funeral Procession, November 1963

President John Fitzgerald Kennedy

Special Message to Congress

May 25, 1961
The Capitol, Washington, D.C.

Mr. Speaker, Mr. Vice President, my co-partners in Government, gentlemen and ladies:

The Constitution imposes upon me the obligation to "from time to time give to the Congress information of the State of the Union." While this has traditionally been interpreted as an annual affair, this tradition has been broken in extraordinary times.

These are extraordinary times. And we face an extraordinary challenge. Our strength as well as our convictions have imposed upon this nation the role of leader in freedom's cause.

No role in history could be more difficult or more important. We stand for freedom.

That is our conviction for ourselves--that is our only commitment to others. No friend, no neutral and no adversary should think otherwise. We are not against any man--or any nation--or any system--except as it is hostile to freedom. Nor am I here to present a new military doctrine, bearing any one name or aimed at any one area. I am here to promote the freedom doctrine.

I.

The great battleground for the defense and expansion of freedom today is the whole southern half of the globe--Asia, Latin America, Africa and the Middle East--the lands of the rising peoples. Their revolution is the greatest in human history.

They seek an end to injustice, tyranny, and exploitation. More than an end, they seek a beginning.

And theirs is a revolution which we would support regardless of the Cold War, and regardless of which political or economic route they should choose to freedom.

For the adversaries of freedom did not create the revolution; nor did they create the conditions which compel it. But they are seeking to ride the crest of its wave--to capture it for themselves.

Yet their aggression is more often concealed than open. They have fired no missiles; and their troops are seldom seen. They send arms, agitators, aid, technicians and propaganda to every troubled area. But where fighting is required, it is usually done by others--by guerrillas striking at night, by assassins striking alone--assassins who have taken the lives of four thousand civil officers in the last twelve months in Vietnam alone--by subversives and saboteurs and insurrectionists, who in some cases control whole areas inside of independent nations.

[At this point the following paragraph, which appears in the text as signed and transmitted to the Senate and House of Representatives, was omitted in the reading of the message:

They possess a powerful intercontinental striking force, large forces for conventional war, a well-trained underground in nearly every country, the power to conscript talent and manpower for any purpose, the capacity for quick decisions, a closed society without dissent or free information, and long experience in the techniques of violence and subversion.

They make the most of their scientific successes, their economic progress and their pose as a foe of colonialism and friend of popular revolution. They prey on unstable or unpopular governments, unsealed, or unknown boundaries, unfilled hopes, convulsive change, massive poverty, illiteracy, unrest and frustration.]

With these formidable weapons, the adversaries of freedom plan to consolidate their territory--to exploit, to control, and finally to destroy the hopes of the world's newest nations; and they have ambition to do it before the end of this decade. It is a contest of will and purpose as well as force and violence--a battle for minds and souls as well as lives and territory. And in that contest, we cannot stand aside.

We stand, as we have always stood from our earliest beginnings, for the independence and equality of all nations. This nation was born of revolution and raised in freedom. And we do not intend to leave an open road for despotism.

There is no single simple policy which meets this challenge. Experience has taught us that no one nation has the power or the wisdom to solve all the problems of the world or manage its revolutionary tides--that extending our commitments does not always increase our security--that any initiative carries with it the risk of a temporary defeat--that nuclear weapons cannot prevent subversion--that no free people can be kept free without will and energy of their own--and that no two nations or situations are exactly alike.

Yet there is much we can do--and must do. The proposals I bring before you are numerous and varied. They arise from the host of special opportunities and dangers which have become increasingly clear in recent months. Taken together, I believe that they can mark another step forward in our effort as a people. I am here to ask the help of this Congress and the nation in approving these necessary measures.

II. ECONOMIC AND SOCIAL PROGRESS AT HOME

The first and basic task confronting this nation this year was to turn recession into recovery. An affirmative anti-recession program, initiated with your cooperation, supported the natural forces in the private sector; and our economy is now enjoying renewed confidence and energy. The recession has been halted. Recovery is under way.

But the task of abating unemployment and achieving a full use of our resources does remain a serious challenge for us all. Large-scale unemployment during a recession is bad enough, but large-scale unemployment during a period of prosperity would be intolerable.

I am therefore transmitting to the Congress a new Manpower Development and Training program, to train or retrain several hundred thousand workers, particularly in those areas where we have seen chronic unemployment as a result of technological factors in new occupational skills over a four-year period, in order to replace those skills made obsolete by automation and industrial change with the new skills which the new processes demand.

It should be a satisfaction to us all that we have made great strides in restoring world confidence in the dollar, halting the outflow of gold and improving our balance of payments. During the last two months, our gold stocks actually increased by seventeen million dollars, compared to a loss of 635 million dollars during the last two months of 1960. We must maintain this progress--and this will require the cooperation and restraint of everyone. As recovery progresses, there will be temptations to seek unjustified price and wage increases. These we cannot afford. They will only handicap our efforts to compete abroad and to achieve full recovery here at home. Labor and management must--and I am confident that they will--pursue responsible wage and price policies in these critical times. I look to the President's Advisory Committee on Labor Management Policy to give a strong lead in this direction.

Moreover, if the budget deficit now increased by the needs of our security is to be held within manageable proportions, it will be necessary to hold tightly to prudent fiscal standards; and I request the cooperation of the Congress in this regard--to refrain from adding funds or programs, desirable as they may be, to the Budget-- to end the postal deficit, as my predecessor also recommended, through increased rates--a deficit incidentally, this year, which exceeds the fiscal 1962 cost of all the space and defense measures that I am submitting today--to provide full pay-as-you-go highway financing--and to close those tax loopholes earlier specified. Our security and progress cannot be cheaply purchased; and their price must be found in what we all forego as well as what we all must pay.

III. ECONOMIC AND SOCIAL PROGRESS ABROAD

I stress the strength of our economy because it is essential to the strength of our nation. And what is true in our case is true in the case of other countries. Their strength in the struggle for freedom depends on the strength of their economic and their social progress.

We would be badly mistaken to consider their problems in military terms alone. For no amount of arms and armies can help stabilize those governments which are unable or unwilling to achieve social and economic reform and development. Military pacts cannot help nations whose social injustice and economic chaos invite insurgency and penetration and subversion. The most skillful counter-guerrilla efforts cannot succeed where the local population is too caught up in its own misery to be concerned about the advance of communism.

But for those who share this view, we stand ready now, as we have in the past, to provide generously of our skills, and our capital, and our food to assist the peoples of the less-developed nations to reach their goals in freedom--to help them before they are engulfed in crisis.

This is also our great opportunity in 1961. If we grasp it, then subversion to prevent its success is exposed as an unjustifiable attempt to keep these nations from either being free or equal. But if we do not pursue it, and if they do not pursue it, the bankruptcy of unstable governments, one by one, and of unfilled hopes will surely lead to a series of totalitarian receiverships.

Earlier in the year, I outlined to the Congress a new program for aiding emerging nations; and it is my intention to transmit shortly draft legislation to implement this program, to establish a new Act for International Development, and to add to the figures previously requested, in view of the swift pace of critical events, an additional 250 million dollars for a Presidential Contingency Fund, to be used only upon a Presidential determination in each case, with regular and complete reports to the Congress in each case, when there is a sudden and extraordinary drain upon our regular funds which we cannot foresee--as illustrated by recent events in Southeast Asia-- and it makes necessary the use of this emergency reserve. The total amount requested--now raised to 2.65 billion dollars--is both minimal and crucial. I do not see how anyone who is concerned--as we all are--about the growing threats to freedom around the globe- -and who is asking what more we can do as a people--can weaken or oppose the single most important program available for building the frontiers of freedom.

IV.

All that I have said makes it clear that we are engaged in a world-wide struggle in which we bear a heavy burden to preserve and promote the ideals that we share with all mankind, or have alien ideals forced upon them. That struggle has highlighted the role of our Information Agency. It is essential that the funds previously requested for this effort be not only approved in full, but increased by 2 million, 400 thousand dollars, to a total of 121 million dollars.

This new request is for additional radio and television to Latin America and Southeast Asia. These tools are particularly effective and essential in the cities and villages of those great continents as a means of reaching millions of uncertain peoples to tell them of our interest in their fight for freedom. In Latin America, we are proposing to increase our Spanish and Portuguese broadcasts to a total of 154 hours a week, compared to 42 hours today, none of which is in Portuguese, the language of about one-third of the people of South America. The Soviets, Red Chinese and satellites already broadcast into Latin America more than 134 hours a week in Spanish and Portuguese. Communist China alone does more public information broadcasting in our own hemisphere than we do. Moreover, powerful propaganda broadcasts from Havana now are heard throughout Latin America, encouraging new revolutions in several countries.

Similarly, in Laos, Vietnam, Cambodia, and Thailand, we must communicate our determination and support to those upon whom our hopes for resisting the communist tide in that continent ultimately depend. Our interest is in the truth.

V. OUR PARTNERSHIP FOR SELF-DEFENSE

But while we talk of sharing and building and the competition of ideas, others talk of arms and threaten war. So we have learned to keep our defenses strong--and to cooperate with others in a partnership of self-defense. The events of recent weeks have caused us to look anew at these efforts.

The center of freedom's defense is our network of world alliances, extending from NATO, recommended by a Democratic President and approved by a Republican Congress, to SEATO, recommended by a Republican President and approved by a Democratic Congress. These alliances were constructed in the 1940's and 1950's--it is our task and responsibility in the 1960's to strengthen them.

To meet the changing conditions of power--and power relationships have changed--we have endorsed an increased emphasis on NATO's conventional strength. At the same time we are affirming our conviction that the NATO nuclear deterrent must also be kept strong. I have made clear our intention to commit to the NATO command, for this purpose, the 5 Polaris submarines originally suggested by President Eisenhower, with the possibility, if needed, of more to come.

Second, a major part of our partnership for self-defense is the Military Assistance Program. The main burden of local defense against local attack, subversion, insurrection or guerrilla warfare must of necessity rest with local forces. Where these forces have the necessary will and capacity to cope with such threats, our intervention is rarely necessary or helpful. Where the will is present and only capacity is lacking, our Military Assistance Program can be of help.

But this program, like economic assistance, needs a new emphasis. It cannot be extended without regard to the social, political and military reforms essential to internal respect and stability. The equipment and training provided must be tailored to legitimate local needs and to our own foreign and military policies, not to our supply of military stocks or a local leader's desire for military display. And military assistance can, in addition to its military purposes, make a contribution to economic progress, as do our own Army Engineers.

In an earlier message, I requested 1.6 billion dollars for Military Assistance, stating that this would maintain existing force levels, but that I could not foresee how much more might be required. It is now clear that this is not enough. The present crisis in Southeast Asia, on which the Vice President has made a valuable report--the rising threat of communism in Latin America--the increased arms traffic in Africa--and all the new pressures on every nation found on the map by tracing your fingers along the borders of the Communist bloc in Asia and the Middle East--all make clear the dimension of our needs.

I therefore request the Congress to provide a total of 1.885 billion dollars for Military Assistance in the coming fiscal year--an amount less than that requested a year ago--but a minimum which must be assured if we are to help those nations make secure their independence. This must be prudently and wisely spent--and that will be our common endeavor. Military and economic assistance has been a heavy burden on our citizens for a long time, and I recognize the strong pressures against it; but this battle is far from over, it is reaching a crucial stage, and I believe we should participate in it. We cannot merely state our opposition to totalitarian advance without paying the price of helping those now under the greatest pressure.

VI. OUR OWN MILITARY AND INTELLIGENCE SHIELD

In line with these developments, I have directed a further reinforcement of our own capacity to deter or resist non-nuclear aggression. In the conventional field, with one exception, I find no present need for large new levies of men. What is needed is rather a change of position to give us still further increases in flexibility.

Therefore, I am directing the Secretary of Defense to undertake a reorganization and modernization of the Army's divisional structure, to increase its non-nuclear firepower, to improve its tactical mobility in any environment, to insure its flexibility to meet any direct or indirect threat, to facilitate its coordination with our major allies, and to provide more modern mechanized divisions in Europe and bring their equipment up to date, and new airborne brigades in both the Pacific and Europe.

And secondly, I am asking the Congress for an additional 100 million dollars to begin the procurement task necessary to re-equip this new Army structure with the most modern material. New helicopters, new armored personnel carriers, and new howitzers, for example, must be obtained now.

Third, I am directing the Secretary of Defense to expand rapidly and substantially, in cooperation with our Allies, the orientation of existing forces for the conduct of non-nuclear war, paramilitary operations and sub-limited or unconventional wars.

In addition our special forces and unconventional warfare units will be increased and reoriented. Throughout the services new emphasis must be placed on the special skills and languages which are required to work with local populations.

Fourth, the Army is developing plans to make possible a much more rapid deployment of a major portion of its highly trained reserve forces. When these plans are completed and the reserve is strengthened, two combat-equipped divisions, plus their supporting forces, a total of 89,000 men, could be ready in an emergency for operations with but 3 weeks' notice--2 more divisions with but 5 weeks' notice--and six additional divisions and their supporting forces, making a total of 10 divisions, could be deployable with less than 8 weeks' notice. In short, these new plans will allow us to almost double the combat power of the Army in less than two months, compared to the nearly nine months heretofore required.

Fifth, to enhance the already formidable ability of the Marine Corps to respond to limited war emergencies, I am asking the Congress for 60 million dollars to increase the Marine Corps strength to 190,000 men. This will increase the initial impact and staying power of our three Marine divisions and three air wings, and provide a trained nucleus for further expansion, if necessary for self-defense.

Finally, to cite one other area of activities that are both legitimate and necessary as a means of self-defense in an age of hidden perils, our whole intelligence effort must be reviewed, and its coordination with other elements of policy assured. The Congress and the American people are entitled to know that we will institute whatever new organization, policies, and control are necessary.

VII. CIVIL DEFENSE

One major element of the national security program which this nation has never squarely faced up to is civil defense. This problem arises not from present trends but from national inaction in which most of us have participated. In the past decade we have intermittently considered a variety of programs, but we have never adopted a consistent policy. Public considerations have been largely characterized by apathy, indifference and skepticism; while, at the same time, many of the civil defense plans have been so far-reaching and unrealistic that they have not gained essential support.

This Administration has been looking hard at exactly what civil defense can and cannot do. It cannot be obtained cheaply. It cannot give an assurance of blast protection that will be proof against surprise attack or guaranteed against obsolescence or destruction. And it cannot deter a nuclear attack.

We will deter an enemy from making a nuclear attack only if our retaliatory power is so strong and so invulnerable that he knows he would be destroyed by our response. If we have that strength, civil defense is not needed to deter an attack. If we should ever lack it, civil defense would not be an adequate substitute.

But this deterrent concept assumes rational calculations by rational men. And the history of this planet, and particularly the history of the 20th century, is sufficient to remind us of the possibilities of an irrational attack, a miscalculation, an accidental war, [or a war of escalation in which the stakes by each side gradually increase to the point of maximum danger] which cannot be either foreseen or deterred. It is on this basis that civil defense can be readily justifiable--as insurance for the civilian population in case of an enemy miscalculation. It is insurance we trust will never be needed--but insurance which we could never forgive ourselves for foregoing in the event of catastrophe.

Once the validity of this concept is recognized, there is no point in delaying the initiation of a nation-wide long-range program of identifying present fallout shelter capacity and providing shelter in new and existing structures. Such a program would protect millions of people against the hazards of radioactive fallout in the event of large-scale nuclear attack. Effective performance of the entire program not only requires new legislative authority and more funds, but also sound organizational arrangements.

Therefore, under the authority vested in me by Reorganization Plan No. 1 of 1958, I am assigning responsibility for this program to the top civilian authority already responsible for continental defense, the Secretary of Defense. It is important that this function remain civilian, in nature and leadership; and this feature will not be changed.

The Office of Civil and Defense Mobilization will be reconstituted as a small staff agency to assist in the coordination of these functions. To more accurately describe its role, its title should be changed to the Office of Emergency Planning.

As soon as those newly charged with these responsibilities have prepared new authorization and appropriation requests, such requests will be transmitted to the Congress for a much strengthened Federal-State civil defense program. Such a program will provide Federal funds for identifying fallout shelter capacity in existing, structures, and it will include, where appropriate, incorporation of shelter in Federal buildings, new requirements for shelter in buildings constructed with Federal assistance, and matching grants and other incentives for constructing shelter in State and local and private buildings.

Federal appropriations for civil defense in fiscal 1962 under this program will in all likelihood be more than triple the pending budget requests; and they will increase sharply in subsequent years. Financial participation will also be required from State and local governments and from private citizens. But no insurance is cost-free; and every American citizen and his community must decide for themselves whether this form of survival insurance justifies the expenditure of effort, time and money. For myself, I am convinced that it does.

VIII. DISARMAMENT

I cannot end this discussion of defense and armaments without emphasizing our strongest hope: the creation of an orderly world where disarmament will be possible. Our aims do not prepare for war--they are efforts to discourage and resist the adventures of others that could end in war.

That is why it is consistent with these efforts that we continue to press for properly safeguarded disarmament measures. At Geneva, in cooperation with the United Kingdom, we have put forward concrete proposals to make clear our wish to meet the Soviets half way in an effective nuclear test ban treaty--the first significant but essential step on the road towards disarmament. Up to now, their response has not been what we hoped, but Mr. Dean returned last night to Geneva, and we intend to go the last mile in patience to secure this gain if we can.

Meanwhile, we are determined to keep disarmament high on our agenda--to make an intensified effort to develop acceptable political and technical alternatives to the present arms race. To this end I shall send to the Congress a measure to establish a strengthened and enlarged Disarmament Agency.

IX. SPACE

Finally, if we are to win the battle that is now going on around the world between freedom and tyranny, the dramatic achievements in space which occurred in recent weeks should have made clear to us all, as did the Sputnik in 1957, the impact of this adventure on the minds of men everywhere, who are attempting to make a determination of which road they should take. Since early in my term, our efforts in space have been under review. With the advice of the Vice President, who is Chairman of the National Space Council, we have examined where we are strong and where we are not, where we may succeed and where we may not. Now it is time to take longer strides--time for a great new American enterprise--time for this nation to take a clearly leading role in space achievement, which in many ways may hold the key to our future on earth.

I believe we possess all the resources and talents necessary. But the facts of the matter are that we have never made the national decisions or marshalled the national resources required for such leadership. We have never specified long-range goals on an urgent time schedule, or managed our resources and our time so as to insure their fulfillment.

Recognizing the head start obtained by the Soviets with their large rocket engines, which gives them many months of leadtime, and recognizing the likelihood that they will exploit this lead for some time to come in still more impressive successes, we nevertheless are required to make new efforts on our own. For while we cannot guarantee that we shall one day be first, we can guarantee that any failure to make this effort will make us last. We take an additional risk by making it in full view of the world, but as shown by the feat of astronaut Shepard, this very risk enhances our stature when we are successful. But this is not merely a race. Space is open to us now; and our eagerness to share its meaning is not governed by the efforts of others. We go into space because whatever mankind must undertake, free men must fully share.

I therefore ask the Congress, above and beyond the increases I have earlier requested for space activities, to provide the funds which are needed to meet the following national goals:

First, I believe that this nation should commit itself to achieving the goal, before this decade is out, of landing a man on the moon and returning him safely to the earth. No single space project in this period will be more impressive to mankind, or more important for the long-range exploration of space; and none will be so difficult or expensive to accomplish. We propose to accelerate the development of the appropriate lunar space craft. We propose to develop alternate liquid and solid fuel boosters, much larger than any now being developed, until certain which is superior. We propose additional funds for other engine development and for unmanned explorations--explorations which are particularly important for one purpose which this nation will never overlook: the survival of the man who first makes this daring flight. But in a very real sense, it will not be one man going to the moon--if we make this judgment affirmatively, it will be an entire nation. For all of us must work to put him there.

Secondly, an additional 23 million dollars, together with 7 million dollars already available, will accelerate development of the Rover nuclear rocket. This gives promise of some day providing a means for even more exciting and ambitious exploration of space, perhaps beyond the moon, perhaps to the very end of the solar system itself.

Third, an additional 50 million dollars will make the most of our present leadership, by accelerating the use of space satellites for world-wide communications.

Fourth, an additional 75 million dollars--of which 53 million dollars is for the Weather Bureau--will help give us at the earliest possible time a satellite system for world-wide weather observation.

Let it be clear--and this is a judgment which the Members of the Congress must finally make--let it be clear that I am asking the Congress and the country to accept a firm commitment to a new course of action, a course which will last for many years and carry very heavy costs: 531 million dollars in fiscal '62--an estimated seven to nine billion dollars additional over the next five years. If we are to go only half way, or reduce our sights in the face of difficulty, in my judgment it would be better not to go at all.

Now this is a choice which this country must make, and I am confident that under the leadership of the Space Committees of the Congress, and the Appropriating Committees, that you will consider the matter carefully.

It is a most important decision that we make as a nation. But all of you have lived through the last four years and have seen the significance of space and the adventures in space, and no one can predict with certainty what the ultimate meaning will be of mastery of space.

I believe we should go to the moon. But I think every citizen of this country as well as the Members of the Congress should consider the matter carefully in making their judgment, to which we have given attention over many weeks and months, because it is a heavy burden, and there is no sense in agreeing or desiring that the United States take an affirmative position in outer space, unless we are prepared to do the work and bear the burdens to make it successful. If we are not, we should decide today and this year.

This decision demands a major national commitment of scientific and technical manpower, materiel and facilities, and the possibility of their diversion from other important activities where they are already thinly spread. It means a degree of dedication, organization and discipline which have not always characterized our research and development efforts. It means we cannot afford undue work stoppages, inflated costs of material or talent, wasteful interagency rivalries, or a high turnover of key personnel.

New objectives and new money cannot solve these problems. They could in fact, aggravate them further--unless every scientist, every engineer, every serviceman, every technician, contractor, and civil servant gives his personal pledge that this nation will move forward, with the full speed of freedom, in the exciting adventure of space.

X. CONCLUSION

In conclusion, let me emphasize one point. It is not a pleasure for any President of the United States, as I am sure it was not a pleasure for my predecessors, to come before the Congress and ask for new appropriations which place burdens on our people. I came to this conclusion with some reluctance. But in my judgment, this is a most serious time in the life of our country and in the life of freedom around the globe, and it is the obligation, I believe, of the President of the United States to at least make his recommendations to the Members of the Congress, so that they can reach their own conclusions with that judgment before them. You must decide yourselves, as I have decided, and I am confident that whether you finally decide in the way that I have decided or not, that your judgment--as my judgment--is reached on what is in the best interests of our country.

In conclusion, let me emphasize one point: that we are determined, as a nation in 1961 that freedom shall survive and succeed--and whatever the peril and set-backs, we have some very large advantages.

The first is the simple fact that we are on the side of liberty--and since the beginning of history, and particularly since the end of the Second World War, liberty has been winning out all over the globe.

A second real asset is that we are not alone. We have friends and allies all over the world who share our devotion to freedom. May I cite as a symbol of traditional and effective friendship the great ally I am about to visit--France. I look forward to my visit to France, and to my discussion with a great Captain of the Western World, President de Gaulle, as a meeting of particular significance, permitting the kind of close and ranging consultation that will strengthen both our countries and serve the common purposes of world-wide peace and liberty. Such serious conversations do not require a pale unanimity--they are rather the instruments of trust and understanding over a long road.

A third asset is our desire for peace. It is sincere, and I believe the world knows it. We are proving it in our patience at the test ban table, and we are proving it in the UN where our efforts have been directed to maintaining that organization's usefulness as a protector of the independence of small nations. In these and other instances, the response of our opponents has not been encouraging.

Yet it is important to know that our patience at the bargaining table is nearly inexhaustible, though our credulity is limited that our hopes for peace are unfailing, while our determination to protect our security is resolute. For these reasons I have long thought it wise to meet with the Soviet Premier for a personal exchange of views. A meeting in Vienna turned out to be convenient for us both; and the Austrian government has kindly made us welcome. No formal agenda is planned and no negotiations will be undertaken; but we will make clear America's enduring concern is for both peace and freedom--that we are anxious to live in harmony with the

Russian people--that we seek no conquests, no satellites, no riches--that we seek only the day when "nation shall not lift up sword against nation, neither shall they learn war any more."

Finally, our greatest asset in this struggle is the American people--their willingness to pay the price for these programs--to understand and accept a long struggle--to share their resources with other less fortunate people--to meet the tax levels and close the tax loopholes I have requested--to exercise self-restraint instead of pushing up wages or prices, or over-producing certain crops, or spreading military secrets, or urging unessential expenditures or improper monopolies or harmful work stoppages--to serve in the Peace Corps or the Armed Services or the Federal Civil Service or the Congress--to strive for excellence in their schools, in their cities and in their physical fitness and that of their children--to take part in Civil Defense--to pay higher postal rates, and higher payroll taxes and higher teachers' salaries, in order to strengthen our society--to show friendship to students and visitors from other lands who visit us and go back in many cases to be the future leaders, with an image of America--and I want that image, and I know you do, to be affirmative and positive--and, finally, to practice democracy at home, in all States, with all races, to respect each other and to protect the Constitutional rights of all citizens.

I have not asked for a single program which did not cause one or all Americans some inconvenience, or some hardship, or some sacrifice. But they have responded and you in the Congress have responded to your duty--and I feel confident in asking today for a similar response to these new and larger demands. It is heartening to know, as I journey abroad, that our country is united in its commitment to freedom and is ready to do its duty.

Berlin Crisis Address

July 25, 1961
The White House, Washington, D.C.

GOOD EVENING:

Seven weeks ago tonight I returned from Europe to report on my meeting with Premier Khrushchev and the others. His grim warnings about the future of the world, his aide memoire on Berlin, his subsequent speeches and threats which he and his agents have launched, and the increase in the Soviet military budget that he has announced, have all prompted a series of decisions by the Administration and a series of consultations with the members of the NATO organization. In Berlin, as you recall, he intends to bring to an end, through a stroke of the pen, *first* our legal rights to be in West Berlin --and *secondly* our ability to make good on our commitment to the two million free people of that city. That we cannot permit.

We are clear about what must be done--and we intend to do it. I want to talk frankly with you tonight about the first steps that we shall take. These actions will require sacrifice on the part of many of our citizens. More will be required in the future. They will require, from all of us, courage and perseverance in the years to come. But if we and our allies act out of strength and unity of purpose--with calm determination and steady nerves--using restraint in our words as well as our weapons--I am hopeful that both peace and freedom will be sustained.

The immediate threat to free men is in West Berlin. But that isolated outpost is not an isolated problem. The threat is worldwide. Our effort must be equally wide and strong, and not be obsessed by any single manufactured crisis. We face a challenge in Berlin, but there is also a challenge in Southeast Asia, where the borders are less guarded, the enemy harder to find, and the dangers of communism less apparent to those who have so little. We face a challenge in our own hemisphere, and indeed wherever else the freedom of human beings is at stake.

Let me remind you that the fortunes of war and diplomacy left the free people of West Berlin, in 1945, 110 miles behind the Iron Curtain.

This map makes very clear the problem that we face. The white is West Germany--the East is the area controlled by the Soviet Union, and as you can see from the chart, West Berlin is 110 miles within the area which the Soviets now dominate--which is immediately controlled by the so-called East German regime.

We are there as a result of our victory over Nazi Germany--and our basic rights to be there, deriving from that victory, include both our presence in West Berlin and the enjoyment of access across East Germany. These rights have been repeatedly confirmed and recognized in special agreements with the Soviet Union. Berlin is not a part of East Germany, but a separate territory under the control of the allied powers. Thus our rights there arc clear and deep-rooted. But in addition to those rights is our commitment to sustain--and defend, if need be--the opportunity for more than two million people to determine their own future and choose their own way of life.

II.

Thus, our presence in West Berlin, and our access thereto, cannot be ended by any act of the Soviet government. The NATO shield was long ago extended to cover West Berlin--and we have given our word that an attack upon that city will be regarded as an attack upon us all.

For West Berlin--lying exposed 110 miles inside East Germany, surrounded by Soviet troops and close to Soviet supply lines, has many roles. It is more than a showcase of liberty, a symbol, an island of freedom in a Communist sea. It is even more than a link with the Free World, a beacon of hope behind the Iron Curtain, an escape hatch for refugees.

West Berlin is all of that. But above all it has now become--as never before--the great testing place of Western courage and will, a focal point where our solemn commitments stretching back over the years since 1945, and Soviet ambitions now meet in basic confrontation.

It would be a mistake for others to look upon Berlin, because of its location, as a tempting target. The United States is there; the United Kingdom and France are there; the pledge of NATO is there-- and the people of Berlin are there. It is as secure, in that sense, as the rest of us--for we cannot separate its safety from our own.

I hear it said that West Berlin is militarily untenable. And so was Bastogne. And so, in fact, was Stalingrad. Any dangerous spot is tenable if men--brave men--will make it so.

We do not want to fight--but we have fought before. And others in earlier times have made the same dangerous mistake of assuming that the West was too selfish and too soft and too divided to resist invasions of freedom in other lands. Those who threaten to unleash the forces of war on a dispute over West Berlin should recall the words of the ancient philosopher: "A man who causes fear cannot be free from fear."

We cannot and will not permit the Communists to drive us out of Berlin, either gradually or by force. For the fulfillment of our pledge to that city is essential to the morale and security of Western Germany, to the unity of Western Europe, and to the faith of the entire Free World. Soviet strategy has long been aimed, not merely at Berlin, but at dividing and neutralizing all of Europe, forcing us back on our own shores. We must meet our oft-stated pledge to the free peoples of West Berlin--and maintain our rights and their safety, even in the face of force--in order to maintain the confidence of other free peoples in our word and our resolve. The strength of the alliance on which our security depends is dependent in turn on our willingness to meet our commitments to them.

III.

So long as the Communists insist that they are preparing to end by themselves unilaterally our rights in West Berlin and our commitments to its people, we must be prepared to defend those rights and those commitments. We will at all times be ready to talk, if talk will help. But we must also be ready to resist with force, if force is used upon us. Either alone would fail. Together, they can serve the cause of freedom and peace.

 The new preparations that we shall make to defend the peace are part of the long-term build-up in our strength which has been underway since January. They are based on our needs to meet a world-wide threat, on a basis which stretches far beyond the present Berlin crisis. Our primary purpose is neither propaganda nor provocation--but preparation.

A first need is to hasten progress toward the military goals which the North Atlantic allies have set for themselves. In Europe today nothing less will suffice. We will put even greater resources into fulfilling those goals, and we look to our allies to do the same.

The supplementary defense build-ups that I asked from the Congress in March and May have already started moving us toward these and our other defense goals. They included an increase in the size of the Marine Corps, improved readiness of our reserves, expansion of our air and sea lift, and stepped-up procurement of needed weapons, ammunition, and other items. To insure a continuing invulnerable capacity to deter or destroy any aggressor, they provided for the strengthening of our missile power and for putting 50% of our B-52 and B-47 bombers on a ground alert which would send them on their way with 15 minutes' warning.

These measures must be speeded up, and still others must now be taken. We must have sea and air lift capable of moving our forces quickly and in large numbers to any part of the world.

But even more importantly, we need the capability of placing in any critical area at the appropriate time a force which, combined with those of our allies, is large enough to make clear our determination and our ability to defend our rights at all costs--and to meet all levels of aggressor pressure with whatever levels of force are required. We intend to have a wider choice than humiliation or all-out nuclear action.

While it is unwise at this time either to call up or send abroad excessive numbers of these troops before they are needed, let me make it clear that I intend to take, as time goes on, whatever steps are necessary to make certain that such forces can be deployed at the appropriate time without lessening our ability to meet our commitments elsewhere.

Thus, in the days and months ahead, I shall not hesitate to ask the Congress for additional measures, or exercise any of the executive powers that I possess to meet this threat to peace. Everything essential to the security of freedom must be done; and if that should require more men, or more taxes, or more controls, or other new powers, I shall not hesitate to ask them. The measures proposed today will be constantly studied, and altered as necessary. But while we will not let panic shape our policy, neither will we permit timidity to direct our program.

Accordingly, I am now taking the following steps:

(1) I am tomorrow requesting the Congress for the current fiscal year an additional $3,247,000,000 of appropriations for the Armed Forces.

(2) To fill out our present Army Divisions, and to make more men available for prompt deployment, I am requesting an increase in the Army's total authorized strength from 875,000 to approximately I million   men.

(3) 1 am requesting an increase of 29,000 and 63,000 men respectively in the active duty strength of the Navy and the Air Force.

(4) To fulfill these manpower needs, I am ordering that our draft calls be doubled and tripled in the coming months; I am asking the Congress for authority to order to active duty certain ready reserve units and individual reservists, and to extend tours of duty; and, under that authority, I am planning to order to active duty a number of air transport squadrons and Air National Guard tactical air squadrons, to give us the airlift capacity and protection that we need. Other reserve forces will be called up when needed.

(5) Many ships and planes once headed for retirement are to be retained or reactivated, increasing our air power tactically and our sealift, airlift, and anti-submarine warfare capability. In addition, our strategic air power will be increased by delaying the deactivation of B-47 bombers.

(6) Finally, some $1.8 billion--about half of the total sum--is needed for the procurement of non-nuclear weapons, ammunition and equipment.

The details on all these requests will be presented to the Congress tomorrow. Subsequent steps will be taken to suit subsequent needs. Comparable efforts for the common defense are being discussed with our NATO allies. For their commitment and interest are as precise as our own.

And let me add that I am well aware of the fact that many American families will bear the burden of these requests. Studies or careers will be interrupted; husbands and sons will be called away; incomes in some cases will be reduced. But these are burdens which must be borne if freedom is to be defended--Americans have willingly borne them before--and they will not flinch from the task now.

IV.

We have another sober responsibility. To recognize the possibilities of nuclear war in the missile age, without our citizens knowing what they should do and where they should go if bombs begin to fall, would be a failure of responsibility. In May, I pledged a new start on Civil Defense. Last week, I assigned, on the recommendation of the Civil Defense Director, basic responsibility for this program to the Secretary of Defense, to make certain it is administered and coordinated with our continental defense efforts at the highest civilian level. Tomorrow, I am requesting of the Congress new funds for the following immediate objectives: to identify and mark space in existing structures--public and private--that could be used for fall-out shelters in case of attack; to stock those shelters with food, water, first-aid kits and other minimum essentials for survival; to increase their capacity; to improve our air-raid warning and fallout detection systems, including a new household warning system which is now under development; and to take other measures that will be effective at an early date to save millions of lives if needed.

In the event of an attack, the lives of those families which are not hit in a nuclear blast and fire can still be saved--if they can be warned to take shelter and if that shelter is available. We owe that kind of insurance to our families--and to our country. In contrast to our friends in Europe, the need for this kind of protection is new to our shores. But the time to start is now. In the coming months, I hope to let every citizen know what steps he can take without delay to protect his family in case of attack. I know that you will want to do no less.

V.

The addition of $207 million in Civil Defense appropriations brings our total new defense budget requests to $3.454 billion, and a total of $47.5 billion for the year. This is an increase in the defense budget of $6 billion since January, and has resulted in official estimates of a budget deficit of over $5 billion. The Secretary of the Treasury and other economic advisers assure me, however, that our economy has the capacity to bear this new request.

We are recovering strongly from this year's recession. The increase in this last quarter of our year of our total national output was greater than that for any postwar period of initial recovery. And yet, wholesale prices are actually lower than they were during the recession, and consumer prices are only 1/4 of 1% higher than they were last October. In fact, this last quarter was the first in eight years in which our production has increased without an increase in the overall-price index. And for the first time since the fall of 1959, our gold position has improved and the dollar is more respected abroad. These gains, it should be stressed, are being accomplished with Budget deficits far smaller than those of the 1958 recession.

This improved business outlook means improved revenues; and I intend to submit to the Congress in January a budget for the next fiscal year which will be strictly in balance. Nevertheless, should an increase in taxes be needed--because of events in the next few months--to achieve that balance, or because of subsequent defense rises, those increased taxes will be requested in January.

Meanwhile, to help make certain that the current deficit is held to a safe level, we must keep down all expenditures not thoroughly justified in budget requests. The luxury of our current post-office deficit must be ended. Costs in military procurement will be closely scrutinized--and in this effort I welcome the cooperation of the Congress. The tax loopholes I have specified--on expense accounts, overseas income, dividends, interest, cooperatives and others-- must be closed.

I realize that no public revenue measure is welcomed by everyone. But I am certain that every American wants to pay his fair share, and not leave the burden of defending freedom entirely to those who bear arms. For we have mortgaged our very future on this defense--and we cannot fail to meet our responsibilities.

VI.

But I must emphasize again that the choice is not merely between resistance and retreat, between atomic holocaust and surrender. Our peace-time military posture is traditionally defensive; but our diplomatic posture need not be. Our response to the Berlin crisis will not be merely military or negative. It will be more than merely standing firm. For we do not intend to leave it to others to choose and monopolize the forum and the framework of discussion. We do not intend to abandon our duty to mankind to seek a peaceful solution.As signers of the UN Charter, we shall always be prepared to discuss international problems with any and all nations that are willing to talk--and listen--with reason. If they have proposals--not demands--we shall hear them. If they seek genuine understanding-- not concessions of our rights--we shall meet with them. We have previously indicated our readiness to remove any actual irritants in West Berlin, but the freedom of that city is riot negotiable. We cannot negotiate with those who say "What's mine is mine and what's yours is negotiable." But we are willing to consider any arrangement or treaty in Germany consistent with the maintenance of peace and freedom, and with the legitimate security interests of all nations.

We recognize the Soviet Union's historical concern about their security in Central and Eastern Europe, after a series of ravaging invasions, and we believe arrangements can be worked out which will help to meet those concerns, and make it possible for both security and freedom to exist in this troubled area.

For it is not the freedom of West Berlin which is "abnormal" in Germany today, but the situation in that entire divided country. If anyone doubts the legality of our rights in Berlin, we are ready to have it submitted to international adjudication. If anyone doubts the extent to which our presence is desired by the people of West Berlin, compared to East German feelings about their regime, we are ready to have that question submitted to a free vote in Berlin and, if possible, among all the German people. And let us hear at that time from the two and one-half million refugees who have fled the Communist regime in East Germany--voting for Western-type freedom with their feet.

The world is not deceived by the Communist attempt to label Berlin as a hot-bed of war. There is peace in Berlin today. The source of world trouble and tension is Moscow, not Berlin. And if war begins, it will have begun in Moscow and not Berlin.

For the choice of peace or war is largely theirs, not ours. It is the Soviets who have stirred up this crisis. It is they who are trying to force a change. It is they who have opposed free elections. It is they who have rejected an all-German peace treaty, and the rulings of international law. And as Americans know from our history on our own old frontier, gun battles are caused by outlaws, and not by officers of the peace.

In short, while we are ready to defend our interests, we shall also be ready to search for peace--in quiet exploratory talks--in formal or informal meetings. We do not want military considerations to dominate the thinking of either East or West., And Mr. Khrushchev may find that his invitation to other nations to join in a meaningless treaty may lead to their inviting him to join in the community of peaceful men, in abandoning the use of force, and in respecting the sanctity of agreements.

While all of these efforts go on, we must not be diverted from our total responsibilities, from other dangers, from other tasks. If new threats in Berlin or elsewhere should cause us to weaken our program of assistance to the developing nations who are also under heavy pressure from the same source, or to halt our efforts for realistic disarmament, or to disrupt or slow down our economy, or to neglect the education of our children, then those threats will surely be the most successful and least costly maneuver in Communist history. For we can afford all these efforts, and more-- but we cannot afford not to meet this challenge.

And the challenge is not to us alone. It is a challenge to every nation which asserts its sovereignty under a system of liberty. It is a challenge to all those who want a world of free choice. It is a special challenge to the Atlantic Community--the heartland of human freedom.

We in the West must move together in building military strength. We must consult one another more closely than ever before. We must together design our proposals for peace, and labor together as they are pressed at the conference table. And together we must share the burdens and the risks of this effort.

The Atlantic Community, as we know it, has been built in response to challenge: the challenge of European chaos in 1947, of the Berlin blockade in 1948, the challenge of Communist aggression in Korea in 1950. Now, standing strong and prosperous, after an unprecedented decade of progress, the Atlantic Community will not forget either its history or the principles which gave it meaning.

The solemn vow each of us gave to West Berlin in time of peace will not be broken in time of danger. If we do not meet our commitments to Berlin, where will we later stand? If we are not true to our word there, all that we have achieved in collective security, which relies on these words, will mean nothing. And if there is one path above all others to war, it is the path of weakness and disunity.

Today, the endangered frontier of freedom runs through divided Berlin. We want it to remain a frontier of peace. This is the hope of every citizen of the Atlantic Community; every citizen of Eastern Europe; and, I am confident, every citizen of the Soviet Union. For I cannot believe that the Russian people--who bravely suffered enormous losses in the Second World War would now wish to see the peace upset once more in Germany. The Soviet government alone can convert Berlin's frontier of peace into a pretext for war.

The steps I have indicated tonight are aimed at avoiding that war. To sum it all up: we seek peace--but we shall not surrender. That is the central meaning of this crisis, and the meaning of your government's policy.

With your help, and the help of other free men, this crisis can be surmounted. Freedom can prevail--and peace can endure.

I would like to close with a personal word. When I ran for the Presidency of the United States, I knew that this country faced serious challenges, but I could not realize--nor could any man realize who does not bear the burdens of this office--how heavy and constant would be those burdens.

Three times in my life-time our country and Europe have been involved in major wars. In each case serious misjudgments were made on both sides of the intentions of others, which brought about great devastation.

Now, in the thermonuclear age, any misjudgment on either side about the intentions of the other could rain more devastation in several hours than has been wrought in all the wars of human history.

Therefore I, as President and Commander-in-Chief, and all of us as Americans, are moving through serious days. I shall bear this responsibility under our Constitution for the next three and one-half .years, but I am sure that we all, regardless of our occupations, will do our very best for our country, and for our cause. For all of us want to see our children grow up in a country at peace, and in a world where freedom endures.

I know that sometimes we get impatient, we wish for some immediate action that would end our perils. But I must tell you that there is no quick and easy solution. The Communists control over a billion people, and they recognize that if we should falter, their success would be imminent.

We must look to long days ahead, which if we are courageous and persevering can bring us what we all desire.

In these days and weeks I ask for your help, and your advice. I ask for your suggestions, when you think we could do better.

All of us, I know, love our country, and we shall all do our best to serve it.

In meeting my responsibilities in these coming months as President, I need your good will, and your support--and above all, your prayers.

Thank you, and good night.

Yale University Commencement Address

June 11, 1962
New Haven, Connecticut

President Griswold, members of the faculty and fellows, graduates and their families, ladies and gentlemen:

Let me begin by expressing my appreciation for the very deep honor which you have conferred upon me. As General de Gaulle occasionally acknowledges America to be the daughter of Europe, so I am pleased to come to Yale, the daughter of Harvard. It might be said now that I have the best of both worlds, a Harvard education and a Yale degree.

I am particularly glad to become a Yale man because as I think about my troubles, I find that a lot of them come from other Yale men. Among businessmen I have had a minor disagreement with Roger Blough of the law school class of 1931, and I have had some complaints from my friend Henry Ford of the class of 1940. In journalism I seem to have a difference with John Hay Whitney, of the class of 1926--and sometimes I also displease Henry Luce of the class of 1920, not to mention also William F. Buckley, Jr. of the class of 1950. I even have some trouble with my Yale advisers. I get along with them, but I am not always sure how they get along with each other.

I have the warmest feelings for Chester Bowles of the class of 1924, and for Dean Acheson of the class of 1915, and my assistant, McGeorge Bundy, of the class of 1940. But I am not 100 percent sure that these three wise and experienced Yale men wholly agree with each other on every issue.

So this administration which aims for peaceful cooperation among all Americans has been the victim of a certain natural pugnacity developed in this city among Yale men. Now that I, too, am a Yale man, it is time for peace. Last week at West Point, in the historic tradition of that Academy, I availed myself of the powers of the Commander in Chief to remit all sentences of offending cadets. In that same spirit, and in the historic tradition of Yale, let me now offer to smoke the clay pipe of friendship with all my brother Elis, and I hope that they may be friends not only with me but even with each other.

In any event, I am very glad to be here and as a new member of the club, I have been checking to see what earlier links existed between the institution of the Presidency and Yale. I found that a member of the class of 1878, William Howard Taft, served one term in the White House as preparation for becoming a member of this faculty. And a graduate of 1804, John C. Calhoun, regarded the Vice Presidency, quite naturally, as too lowly a status for a Yale alumnus--and became the only man in history to ever resign that office.

Calhoun in 1804 and Taft in 1878 graduated into a world very different from ours today. They and their contemporaries spent entire careers stretching over 40 years in grappling with a few dramatic issues on which the Nation was sharply and emotionally divided, issues that occupied the attention of a generation at a time: the national bank, the disposal of the public lands, nullification or union, freedom or slavery, gold or silver. Today these old sweeping issues very largely have disappeared. The central domestic issues of our time are more subtle and less simple. They relate not to basic clashes of philosophy or ideology but to ways and means of reaching common goals--to research for sophisticated solutions to complex and obstinate issues. The world of Calhoun, the world of Taft had its own hard problems and notable challenges. But its problems are not our problems. Their age is not our age. As every past generation has had to disenthrall itself from an inheritance of truisms and stereotypes, so in our own time we must move on from the reassuring repetition of stale phrases to a new, difficult, but essential confrontation with reality.

For the great enemy of truth is very often not the lie--deliberate, contrived and dishonest--but the myth--persistent, persuasive, and unrealistic. Too often we hold fast to the cliches of our forebears. We subject all facts to a prefabricated set of interpretations. We enjoy the comfort of opinion without the discomfort of thought.

Mythology distracts us everywhere--in government as in business, in politics as in economics, in foreign affairs as in domestic affairs. But today I want to particularly consider the myth and reality in our national economy. In recent months many have come to feel, as I do, that the dialog between the parties--between business and government, between the government and the public--is clogged by illusion and platitude and fails to reflect the true realities of contemporary American society.

I speak of these matters here at Yale because of the self-evident truth that a great university is always enlisted against the spread of illusion and on the side of reality. No one has said it more clearly than your President Griswold: "Liberal learning is both a safeguard against false ideas of freedom and a source of true ones." Your role as university men, whatever your calling, will be to increase each new generation's grasp of its duties.

There are three great areas of our domestic affairs in which, today, there is a danger that illusion may prevent effective action. They are, first, the question of the size and the shape of the government's responsibilities; second, the question of public fiscal policy; and third, the matter of confidence, business confidence or public confidence, or simply confidence in America. I want to talk about all three, and I want to talk about them carefully and dispassionately--and I emphasize that I am concerned here not with political debate but with finding ways to separate false problems from real ones.

If a contest in angry argument were forced upon it, no administration could shrink from response, and history does not suggest that American Presidents are totally without resources in an engagement forced upon them because of hostility in one sector of society. But in the wider national interest, we need not partisan wrangling but common concentration on common problems. I come here to this distinguished university to ask you to join in this great task.

Let us take first the question of the size and shape of government. The myth here is that government is big, and bad--and steadily getting bigger and worse. Obviously this myth has some excuse for existence. It is true that in recent history each new administration has spent much more money than its predecessor. Thus President Roosevelt outspent President Hoover, and with allowances for the special case of the Second World War, President Truman outspent President Roosevelt. Just to prove that this was not a partisan matter, President Eisenhower then outspent President Truman by the handsome figure of $182 billion. It is even possible, some think, that this trend will continue.

But does it follow from this that big government is growing relatively bigger? It does not--for the fact is for the last 15 years, the Federal Government--and also the Federal debt--and also the Federal bureaucracy--have grown less rapidly than the economy as a whole. If we leave defense and space expenditures aside, the Federal Government since the Second World War has expanded less than any other major sector of our national life--less than industry, less than commerce, less than agriculture, less than higher education, and very much less than the noise about big government.

The truth about big government is the truth about any other great activity--it is complex. Certainly it is true that size brings dangers- - but it is also true that size can bring benefits. Here at Yale which has contributed so much to our national progress in science and medicine, it may be proper for me to note one great and little noticed expansion of government which has brought strength to our whole society-- the new role of our Federal Government as the major patron of research in science and in medicine. Few people realize that in 1961, in support of all university research in science and medicine, three dollars out of every four came from the Federal Government. I need hardly point out that this has taken place without undue enlargement of Government control--that American scientists remain second to none in their independence and in their individualism.

I am not suggesting that Federal expenditures cannot bring some measure of control. The whole thrust of Federal expenditures in agriculture have been related by purpose and design to control, as a means of dealing with the problems created by our farmers and our growing productivity. Each sector, my point is, of activity must be approached on its own merits and on terms of specific national needs. Generalities in regard to Federal expenditures, therefore, can be misleading--each case, science, urban renewal, education, agriculture, natural resources, each case must be determined on its merits if we are to profit from our unrivaled ability to combine the strength of public and private purpose.

Next, let us turn to the problem of our fiscal policy. Here the myths are legion and the truth hard to find. But let me take as a prime example the problem of the Federal budget. We persist in measuring our Federal fiscal integrity today by the conventional or administrative budget--with results which would be considered absurd in any business firm--in any country of Europe--or in any careful assessment of the reality of our national finances. The administrative budget has sound administrative uses. But for wider purposes it is less helpful. It omits our special trust funds and the effect they have on our economy; it neglects changes in assets and inventories. It cannot tell a loan from a straight expenditure--and worst of all it cannot distinguish between operating expenditures and long term investments.

This budget, in relation to the great problems of Federal fiscal policy which are basic to our economy in 1962, is not simply irrelevant; it can be actively misleading. And yet there is a mythology that measures all of our national soundness or unsoundness on the single simple basis of this same annual administrative budget. If our Federal budget is to serve not the debate but the country, we must and will find ways of clarifying this area of discourse.

Still in the area of fiscal policy, let me say a word about deficits. The myth persists that Federal deficits create inflation and budget surpluses prevent it. Yet sizeable budget surpluses after the war did not prevent inflation, and persistent deficits for the last several years have not upset our basic price stability. Obviously deficits are sometimes dangerous--and so are surpluses. But honest assessment plainly requires a more sophisticated view than the old and automatic cliche that deficits automatically bring inflation.

There are myths also about our public debt. It is widely supposed that this debt is growing at a dangerously rapid rate. In fact, both the debt per person and the debt as a proportion of our national product have declined sharply since the Second World War. In absolute terms the national debt since the end of World War II has increased only 8 percent, while private debt was increasing 305 percent, and the debts of state and local governments--on whom people frequently suggest we should place additional burdens--the debts of state and local governments have increased 378 percent. Moreover, debts public and private, are neither good nor bad, in and of themselves. Borrowing can lead to over-extension and collapse--but it can also lead to expansion and strength. There is no single, simple slogan in this field that we can trust.

Finally, I come to the matter of confidence. Confidence is a matter of myth and also a matter of truth--and this time let me make the truth of the matter first.

It is true--and of high importance--that the prosperity of this country depends on the assurance that all major elements within it will live up to their responsibilities. If business were to neglect its obligations to the public, if labor were blind to all public responsibility, above all, if government were to abandon its obvious--and statutory--duty of watchful concern for our economical health--if any of these things should happen, then confidence might well be weakened and the danger of stagnation would increase. This is the true issue of confidence.

But there is also the false issue--and its simplest form is the assertion that any and all of the unfavorable turns of the speculative wheel--however temporary and however plainly speculative in character-- are the result of, and I quote, "a lack of confidence in the national administration." This I must tell you, while comforting, is not wholly true. Worse, it obscures the reality-- which is also simple. The solid ground of mutual confidence is the necessary partnership of government with all of the sectors of our society in the steady quest for economic progress.

Corporate plans are not based on political confidence in party leaders but on an economic confidence in the Nation's ability to invest and produce and consume. Business had full confidence in the administrations in power in 1929, 1954, 1958, and 1960--but this was not enough to prevent recession when business lacked full confidence in the economy. What matters is the capacity of the Nation as a whole to deal with its economic problems and its opportunities.

The stereotypes I have been discussing distract our attention and divide our effort. These stereotypes do our Nation a disservice, not just because they are exhausted and irrelevant, but above all because they are misleading--because they stand in the way of the solution of hard and complicated facts. It is not new that past debates should obscure present realities. But the damage of such a false dialogue is greater today than ever before simply because today the safety of all the world--the very future of freedom-- depends as never before on the sensible and clearheaded management of the domestic affairs of the United States.

The real issues of our time are rarely as dramatic as the issues of Calhoun. The differences today are usually matters of degree. And we cannot understand and attack our contemporary problems in

1962 if we are bound by traditional labels and worn out slogans of an earlier era. But the unfortunate fact of the matter is that our rhetoric has not kept pace with the speed of social and economic change. Our political debates, our public discourse--on current domestic and economic issues-- too often bear little or no relation to the actual problems the United States faces.

What is at stake in our economic decisions today is not some grand warfare of rival ideologies which will sweep the country with passion, but the practical management of a modern economy. What we need is not labels and cliches but more basic discussion of the sophisticated and technical questions involved in keeping a great economic machinery moving ahead.

The national interest lies in high employment and steady expansion of output, in stable prices and a strong dollar. The declaration of such an objective is easy; their attainment in an intricate and interdependent economy and world is a little more difficult. To attain them, we require not some automatic response but hard thought. Let me end by suggesting a few of the real questions on our national agenda.

First, how can our budget and tax policies supply adequate revenues and preserve our balance of payments position without slowing up our economic growth?

Two, how are we to set our interest rates and regulate the flow of money, in ways which will stimulate the economy at home, without weakening the dollar abroad? Given the spectrum of our domestic and international responsibilities, what should be the mix between fiscal and monetary policy?

Let me give several examples from my experience of the complexity of these matters and how political labels and ideological approaches are irrelevant to the solution.

Last week, a distinguished graduate of this school, Senator Proxmire, of the class of 1938, who is ordinarily regarded as a liberal Democrat, suggested that we should follow in meeting our economic problems a stiff fiscal policy, with emphasis on budget balance and an easy monetary policy with low interest rates in order to keep our economy going. In the same week, the Bank for International Settlement in Basel, Switzerland, a conservative organization representing the central bankers of Europe suggested that the appropriate economic policy in the United States should be the very opposite; that we should follow a flexible budget policy, as in Europe, with deficits when the economy is down and a high monetary policy on interest rates, as in Europe, in order to control inflation and protect goals. Both may be right or wrong. It will depend on many different factors.

The point is that this is basically an administrative or executive problem in which political labels or cliches do not give us a solution.

A well-known business journal this morning, as I journeyed to New Haven, raised the prospects that a further budget deficit would bring inflation and encourage the flow of gold. We have had several budget deficits beginning with a $12 1/2 billion budget deficit in 1958, and it is true that in the fall of 1960 we had a gold dollar loss running at $5 billion annually. This would seem to prove the case that a deficit produces inflation and that we lose gold, yet there was no inflation following the deficit of 1958 nor has there been inflation since then.

Our wholesale price index since 1958 has remained completely level in spite of several deficits, because the loss of gold has been due to other reasons: price instability, relative interest rates, relative export-import balances, national security expenditures--all the rest.

Let me give you a third and final example. At the World Bank meeting in September, a number of American bankers attending predicted to their European colleagues that because of the fiscal 1962 budget deficit, there would be a strong inflationary pressure on the dollar and a loss of gold. Their predictions on inflation were shared by many in business and helped push the market up. The recent reality of noninflation helped bring it down. We have had no inflation because we have had other factors in our economy that have contributed to price stability.

I do not suggest that the government is right and they are wrong. The fact of the matter is in the Federal Reserve Board and in the administration this fall, a similar view was held by many well-informed and disinterested men that inflation was the major problem that we would face in the winter of 1962. But it was not. What I do suggest is that these problems are endlessly complicated and yet they go to the future of this country and its ability to prove to the world what we believe it must prove.

I am suggesting that the problems of fiscal and monetary policies in the sixties as opposed to the kinds of problems we faced in the thirties demand subtle challenges for which technical answers, not political answers, must be provided. These are matters upon which government and business may and in many cases will disagree. They are certainly matters which government and business should be discussing in the most sober, dispassionate and careful way if we are to maintain the kind of vigorous economy upon which our country depends.

How can we develop and sustain strong and stable world markets for basic commodities without unfairness to the consumer and without undue stimulus to the producer? How can we generate the buying power which can consume what we produce on our farms and in our factories? How can we take advantage of the miracles of automation with the great demand that it will put upon highly skilled labor and yet offer employment to the half million of unskilled school dropouts each year who enter the labor market, eight million of them in the 1960's?

How do we eradicate the barriers which separate substantial minorities of our citizens from access to education and employment on equal terms with the rest?

How, in sum, can we make our free economy work at full capacity--that is, provide adequate profits for enterprise, adequate wages for labor, adequate utilization of plant, and opportunity for all?

These are the problems that we should be talking about--that the political parties and the various groups in our country should be discussing. They cannot be solved by incantations from the forgotten past. But the example of Western Europe shows that they are capable of solution--that governments, and many of them are conservative governments, prepared to face technical problems without ideological preconceptions, can coordinate the elements of a national economy, and bring about growth and prosperity--a decade of it.

Some conversations I have heard in our own country sound like old records, long-playing, left over from the middle thirties. The debate of the thirties had its great significance and produced great results, but it took place in a different world with different needs and different tasks. It is our responsibility today to live in our own world, and to identify the needs and discharge the tasks of the 1960's.

If there is any current trend toward meeting present problems with old cliches, this is the moment to stop it--before it lands us all in a bog of sterile acrimony.

Discussion is essential; and I am hopeful that the debate of recent weeks, though up to now somewhat barren, may represent the start of a serious dialog of the kind which has led in Europe to such fruitful collaboration among all the elements of economic society and to a decade of unrivaled economic progress. But let us not engage in the wrong argument at the wrong time between the wrong people in the wrong country--while the real problems of our own time grow and multiply, fertilized by our neglect.

Nearly 150 years ago Thomas Jefferson wrote, "The new circumstances under which we are placed call for new words, new phrases, and for the transfer of old words to new objects." New words, new phrases, the transfer of old words to new objects--that is truer today than it was in the time of Jefferson, because the role of this country is so vastly more significant. There is a show in England called "Stop the World, I Want to Get Off." You have not chosen to exercise that option. You are part of the world and you must participate in these days of our years in the solution of the problems that pour upon us, requiring the most sophisticated and technical judgment; and as we work in consonance to meet the authentic problems of our times, we will generate a vision and an energy which will demonstrate anew to the world the superior vitality and strength of the free society.

National Space Effort Address

September 12, 1962
Rice University, Houston, Texas

President Pitzer, Mr. Vice President, Governor, Congressman Thomas, Senator Wiley, and Congressman Miller, Mr. Webb, Mr. Bell, scientists, distinguished guests, and ladies and gentlemen:

I appreciate your president having made me an honorary visiting professor, and I will assure you that my first lecture will be very brief.

I am delighted to be here and I'm particularly delighted to be here on this occasion.

We meet at a college noted for knowledge, in a city noted for progress, in a State noted for strength, and we stand in need of all three, for we meet in an hour of change and challenge, in a decade of hope and fear, in an age of both knowledge and ignorance. The greater our knowledge increases, the greater our ignorance unfolds.

Despite the striking fact that most of the scientists that the world has ever known are alive and working today, despite the fact that this Nation's own scientific manpower is doubling every 12 years in a rate of growth more than three times that of our population as a whole, despite that, the vast stretches of the unknown and the unanswered and the unfinished still far outstrip our collective comprehension.

No man can fully grasp how far and how fast we have come, but condense, if you will, the 50,000 years of man's recorded history in a time span of but a half a century. Stated in these terms, we know very little about the first 40 years, except at the end of them advanced man had learned to use the skins of animals to cover them. Then about 10 years ago, under this standard, man emerged from his caves to construct other kinds of shelter. Only five years ago man learned to write and use a cart with wheels. Christianity began less than two years ago. The printing press came this year, and then less than two months ago, during this whole 50-year span of human history, the steam engine provided a new source of power.

Newton explored the meaning of gravity. Last month electric lights and telephones and automobiles and airplanes became available. Only last week did we develop penicillin and television and nuclear power, and now if America's new spacecraft succeeds in reaching Venus, we will have literally reached the stars before midnight tonight.

This is a breathtaking pace, and such a pace cannot help but create new ills as it dispels old, new ignorance, new problems, new dangers. Surely the opening vistas of space promise high costs and hardships, as well as high reward.

So it is not surprising that some would have us stay where we are a little longer to rest, to wait. But this city of Houston, this State of Texas, this country of the United States was not built by those who waited and rested and wished to look behind them. This country was conquered by those who moved forward--and so will space.

William Bradford, speaking in 1630 of the founding of the Plymouth Bay Colony, said that all great and honorable actions are accompanied with great difficulties, and both must be enterprised and overcome with answerable courage.

If this capsule history of our progress teaches us anything, it is that man, in his quest for knowledge and progress, is determined and cannot be deterred. The exploration of space will go ahead, whether we join in it or not, and it is one of the great adventures of all time, and no nation which expects to be the leader of other nations can expect to stay behind in the race for space.

Those who came before us made certain that this country rode the first waves of the industrial revolutions, the first waves of modern invention, and the first wave of nuclear power, and this generation does not intend to founder in the backwash of the coming age of space. We mean to be a part of it--we mean to lead it. For the eyes of the world now look into space, to the moon and to the planets beyond, and we have vowed that we shall not see it governed by a hostile flag of conquest, but by a banner of freedom and peace. We have vowed that we shall not see space filled with weapons of mass destruction, but with instruments of knowledge and understanding.

Yet the vows of this Nation can only be fulfilled if we in this Nation are first, and, therefore, we intend to be first. In short, our leadership in science and in industry, our hopes for peace and security, our obligations to ourselves as well as others, all require us to make this effort, to solve these mysteries, to solve them for the good of all men, and to become the world's leading space-faring nation.

We set sail on this new sea because there is new knowledge to be gained, and new rights to be won, and they must be won and used for the progress of all people. For space science, like nuclear science and all technology, has no conscience of its own. Whether it will become a force for good or ill depends on man, and only if the United States occupies a position of pre-eminence can we help decide whether this new ocean will be a sea of peace or a new terrifying theater of war. I do not say the we should or will go unprotected against the hostile misuse of space any more than we go unprotected against the hostile use of land or sea, but I do say that space can be explored and mastered without feeding the fires of war, without repeating the mistakes that man has made in extending his writ around this globe of ours.

There is no strife, no prejudice, no national conflict in outer space as yet. Its hazards are hostile to us all. Its conquest deserves the best of all mankind, and its opportunity for peaceful cooperation many never come again. But why, some say, the moon? Why choose this as our goal? And they may well ask why climb the highest mountain? Why, 35 years ago, fly the Atlantic? Why does Rice play Texas?

We choose to go to the moon. We choose to go to the moon in this decade and do the other things, not because they are easy, but because they are hard, because that goal will serve to organize and measure the best of our energies and skills, because that challenge is one that we are willing to accept, one we are unwilling to postpone, and one which we intend to win, and the others, too.

It is for these reasons that I regard the decision last year to shift our efforts in space from low to high gear as among the most important decisions that will be made during my incumbency in the office of the Presidency.

In the last 24 hours we have seen facilities now being created for the greatest and most complex exploration in man's history. We have felt the ground shake and the air shattered by the testing of a Saturn C-1 booster rocket, many times as powerful as the Atlas which launched John Glenn, generating power equivalent to 10,000 automobiles with their accelerators on the floor. We have seen the site where five F-1 rocket engines, each one as powerful as all eight engines of the Saturn combined, will be clustered together to make the advanced Saturn missile, assembled in a new building to be built at Cape Canaveral as tall as a 48 story structure, as wide as a city block, and as long as two lengths of this field.

Within these last 19 months at least 45 satellites have circled the earth. Some 40 of them were "made in the United States of America" and they were far more sophisticated and supplied far more knowledge to the people of the world than those of the Soviet Union.

The Mariner spacecraft now on its way to Venus is the most intricate instrument in the history of space science. The accuracy of that shot is comparable to firing a missile from Cape Canaveral and dropping it in this stadium between the the 40-yard lines.

Transit satellites are helping our ships at sea to steer a safer course. Tiros satellites have given us unprecedented warnings of hurricanes and storms, and will do the same for forest fires and icebergs.

We have had our failures, but so have others, even if they do not admit them. And they may be less public.

To be sure, we are behind, and will be behind for some time in manned flight. But we do not intend to stay behind, and in this decade, we shall make up and move ahead.

The growth of our science and education will be enriched by new knowledge of our universe and environment, by new techniques of learning and mapping and observation, by new tools and computers for industry, medicine, the home as well as the school. Technical institutions, such as Rice, will reap the harvest of these gains.

And finally, the space effort itself, while still in its infancy, has already created a great number of new companies, and tens of thousands of new jobs. Space and related industries are generating new demands in investment and skilled personnel, and this city and this State, and this region, will share greatly in this growth. What was once the furthest outpost on the old frontier of the West will be the furthest outpost on the new frontier of science and space. Houston, your City of Houston, with its Manned Spacecraft Center, will become the heart of a large scientific and engineering community. During the next 5 years the National Aeronautics and Space Administration expects to double the number of scientists and engineers in this area, to increase its outlays for salaries and expenses to $60 million a year; to invest some $200 million in plant and laboratory facilities; and to direct or contract for new space efforts over $1 billion from this Center in this City.

To be sure, all this costs us all a good deal of money. This year's space budget is three times what it was in January 1961, and it is greater than the space budget of the previous eight years combined. That budget now stands at $5,400 million a year--a staggering sum, though somewhat less than we pay for cigarettes and cigars every year. Space expenditures will soon rise some more, from 40 cents per person per week to more than 50 cents a week for every man, woman and child in the United Stated, for we have given this program a high national priority--even though I realize that this is in some measure an act of faith and vision, for we do not now know what benefits await us. But if I were to say, my fellow citizens, that we shall send to the moon, 240,000 miles away from the control station in Houston, a giant rocket more than 300 feet tall, the length of this football field, made of new metal alloys, some of which have not yet been invented, capable of standing heat and stresses several times more than have ever been experienced, fitted together with a precision better than the finest watch, carrying all the equipment needed for propulsion, guidance, control, communications, food and survival, on an untried mission, to an unknown celestial body, and then return it safely to earth, re-entering the atmosphere at speeds of over 25,000 miles per hour, causing heat about half that of the temperature of the sun--almost as hot as it is here today--and do all this, and do it right, and do it first before this decade is out--then we must be bold.

I'm the one who is doing all the work, so we just want you to stay cool for a minute. [*laughter*]

However, I think we're going to do it, and I think that we must pay what needs to be paid. I don't think we ought to waste any money, but I think we ought to do the job. And this will be done in the decade of the sixties. It may be done while some of you are still here at school at this college and university. It will be done during the term of office of some of the people who sit here on this platform. But it will be done. And it will be done before the end of this decade.

I am delighted that this university is playing a part in putting a man on the moon as part of a great national effort of the United States of America.

Many years ago the great British explorer George Mallory, who was to die on Mount Everest, was asked why did he want to climb it. He said, "Because it is there."

Well, space is there, and we're going to climb it, and the moon and the planets are there, and new hopes for knowledge and peace are there. And, therefore, as we set sail we ask God's blessing on the most hazardous and dangerous and greatest adventure on which man has ever embarked.

Thank you.

The University of Mississippi Address

September 30, 1962
The White House, Washington, D.C.

Good evening my fellow citizens:

The orders of the court in the case of Meredith versus Fair are beginning to be carried out. Mr. James Meredith is now in residence on the campus of the University of Mississippi.

This has been accomplished thus far without the use of National Guard or other troops. And it is to be hoped that the law enforcement officers of the State of Mississippi and the Federal marshals will continue to be sufficient in the future.

All students, members of the faculty, and public officials in both Mississippi and the Nation will be able, it is hoped, to return to their normal activities with full confidence in the integrity of American law.

This is as it should be, for our Nation is founded on the principle that observance of the law is the eternal safeguard of liberty and defiance of the law is the surest road to tyranny. The law which we obey includes the final rulings of the courts, as well as the enactments of our legislative bodies. Even among law-abiding men few laws are universally loved, but they are uniformly respected and not resisted.

Americans are free, in short, to disagree with the law but not to disobey it. For in a government of laws and not of men, no man, however prominent or powerful, and no mob however unruly or boisterous, is entitled to defy a court of law. If this country should ever reach the point where any man or group of men by force or threat of force could long defy the commands of our court and our Constitution, then no law would stand free from doubt, no judge would be sure of his writ, and no citizen would be safe from his neighbors.

In this case in which the United States Government was not until recently involved, Mr. Meredith brought a private suit in Federal court against those who were excluding him from the University. A series of Federal courts all the way to the Supreme Court repeatedly ordered Mr. Meredith's admission to the University. When those orders were defied, and those who sought to implement them were threatened with arrest and violence, the United States Court of Appeals consisting of Chief Judge Tuttle of Georgia, Judge Hutcheson of Texas, Judge Rives of Alabama, Judge Jones of Florida, Judge Brown of Texas, Judge Wisdom of Louisiana, Judge Gewin of Alabama, and Judge Bell of Georgia, made clear the fact that the enforcement of its order had become an obligation of the United States Government. Even though this Government had not originally been a party to the case, my responsibility as President was therefore inescapable. I accept it. My obligation under the Constitution and the statutes of the United States was and is to implement the orders of the court with whatever means are necessary, and with as little force and civil disorder as the circumstances permit.

It was for this reason that I federalized the Mississippi National Guard as the most appropriate instrument, should any be needed, to preserve law and order while United States marshals carried out the orders of the court and prepared to back them up with whatever other civil or military enforcement might have been required.

I deeply regret the fact that any action by the executive branch was necessary in this case, but all other avenues and alternatives, including persuasion and conciliation, had been tried and exhausted. Had the police powers of Mississippi been used to support the orders of the court, instead of deliberately and unlawfully blocking them, had the University of Mississippi fulfilled its standard of excellence by quietly admitting this applicant in conformity with what so many other southern State universities have done for so many years, a peaceable and sensible solution would have been possible without any Federal intervention.

This Nation is proud of the many instances in which Governors, educators, and everyday citizens from the South have shown to the world the gains that can be made by persuasion and good will in a society ruled by law. Specifically, I would like to take this occasion to express the thanks of this Nation to those southerners who have contributed to the progress of our democratic development in the entrance of students regardless of race to such great institutions as the State-supported universities of Virginia, North Carolina, Georgia, Florida, Texas, Louisiana, Tennessee, Arkansas, and Kentucky.

I recognize that the present period of transition and adjustment in our Nation's Southland is a hard one for many people. Neither Mississippi nor any other southern State deserves to be charged with all the accumulated wrongs of the last 100 years of race relations. To the extent that there has been failure, the responsibility for that failure must be shared by us all, by every State, by every citizen.

Mississippi and her University, moreover, are noted for their courage, for their contribution of talent and thought to the affairs of this Nation. This is the State of Lucius Lamar and many others who have placed the national good ahead of sectional interest. This is the State which had four Medal of Honor winners in the Korean War alone. In fact, the Guard unit federalized this morning, early, is part of the 155th Infantry, one of the 10 oldest regiments in the Union and one of the most decorated for sacrifice and bravery in 6 wars.

In 1945 a Mississippi sergeant, Jake Lindsey, was honored by an unusual joint session of the Congress. I close therefore, with this appeal to the students of the University, the people who are most concerned.

You have a great tradition to uphold, a tradition of honor and courage won on the field of battle and on the gridiron as well as the University campus. You have a new opportunity to show that you are men of patriotism and integrity. For the most effective means of upholding the law is not the State policeman or the marshals or the National Guard. It is you. It lies in your courage to accept those laws with which you disagree as well as those with which you agree. The eyes of the Nation and of all the world are upon you and upon all of us, and the honor of your University and State are in the balance. I am certain that the great majority of the students will uphold that honor.

There is in short no reason why the books on this case cannot now be quickly and quietly closed in the manner directed by the court. Let us preserve both the law and the peace and then healing those wounds that are within we can turn to the greater crises that are without and stand united as one people in our pledge to man's freedom.

Thank you and good night.

The Cuban Missile Crisis Address

October 22, 1962
The White House, Washington, D.C.

Good evening my fellow citizens:

This Government, as promised, has maintained the closest surveillance of the Soviet Military buildup on the island of Cuba. Within the past week, unmistakable evidence has established the fact that a series of offensive missile sites is now in preparation on that imprisoned island. The purpose of these bases can be none other than to provide a nuclear strike capability against the Western Hemisphere.

Upon receiving the first preliminary hard information of this nature last Tuesday morning at 9 a.m., I directed that our surveillance be stepped up. And having now confirmed and completed our evaluation of the evidence and our decision on a course of action, this Government feels obliged to report this new crisis to you in fullest detail.

The characteristics of these new missile sites indicate two distinct types of installations. Several of them include medium range ballistic missiles capable of carrying a nuclear warhead for a distance of more than 1,000 nautical miles. Each of these missiles, in short, is capable of striking Washington, D.C., the Panama Canal, Cape Canaveral, Mexico City, or any other city in the southeastern part of the United States, in Central America, or in the Caribbean area.

Additional sites not yet completed appear to be designed for intermediate range ballistic missiles--capable of traveling more than twice as far--and thus capable of striking most of the major cities in the Western Hemisphere, ranging as far north as Hudson Bay, Canada, and as far south as Lima, Peru. In addition, jet bombers, capable of carrying nuclear weapons, are now being uncrated and assembled in Cuba, while the necessary air bases are being prepared.

This urgent transformation of Cuba into an important strategic base--by the presence of these large, long range, and clearly offensive weapons of sudden mass destruction--constitutes an explicit threat to the peace and security of all the Americas, in flagrant and deliberate defiance of the Rio Pact of 1947, the traditions of this Nation and hemisphere, the joint resolution of the 87th Congress, the Charter of the United Nations, and my own public warnings to the Soviets on September 4 and 13. This action also contradicts the repeated assurances of Soviet spokesmen, both publicly and privately delivered, that the arms buildup in Cuba would retain its original defensive character, and that the Soviet Union had no need or desire to station strategic missiles on the territory of any other nation.

The size of this undertaking makes clear that it has been planned for some months. Yet only last month, after I had made clear the distinction between any introduction of ground-to-ground missiles and the existence of defensive antiaircraft missiles, the Soviet Government publicly stated on September 11, and I quote, "the armaments and military equipment sent to Cuba are designed exclusively for defensive purposes," that, and I quote the Soviet Government, "there is no need for the Soviet Government to shift its weapons . . . for a retaliatory blow to any other country, for instance Cuba," and that, and I quote their government, "the Soviet Union has so powerful rockets to carry these nuclear warheads that there is no need to search for sites for them beyond the boundaries of the Soviet Union." That statement was false.

Only last Thursday, as evidence of this rapid offensive buildup was already in my hand, Soviet Foreign Minister Gromyko told me in my office that he was instructed to make it clear once again, as he said his government had already done, that Soviet assistance to Cuba, and I quote, "pursued solely the purpose of contributing to the the defense capabilities of Cuba," that, and I quote him, "training by Soviet specialists of Cuban nationals in handling defensive armaments was by no means offensive, and if it were otherwise," Mr. Gromyko went on, "the Soviet Government would never become involved in rendering such assistance." That statement also was false.

Neither the United States of America nor the world community of nations can tolerate deliberate deception and offensive threats on the part of any nation, large or small. We no longer live in a world where only the actual firing of weapons represents a sufficient challenge to a nation's security to constitute maximum peril. Nuclear weapons are so destructive and ballistic missiles are so swift, that any substantially increased possibility of their use or any sudden change in their deployment may well be regarded as a definite threat to peace.

For many years both the Soviet Union and the United States, recognizing this fact, have deployed strategic nuclear weapons with great care, never upsetting the precarious status quo which insured that these weapons would not be used in the absence of some vital challenge. Our own strategic missiles have never been transferred to the territory of any other nation under a cloak of secrecy and deception; and our history--unlike that of the Soviets since the end of World War II--demonstrates that we have no desire to dominate or conquer any other nation or impose our system upon its people. Nevertheless, American citizens have become adjusted to living daily on the Bull's-eye of Soviet missiles located inside the U.S.S.R. or in submarines.

In that sense, missiles in Cuba add to an already clear and present danger--although it should be noted the nations of Latin America have never previously been subjected to a potential nuclear threat.

But this secret, swift, and extraordinary buildup of Communist missiles--in an area well known to have a special and historical relationship to the United States and the nations of the Western

Hemisphere, in violation of Soviet assurances, and in defiance of American and hemispheric policy--this sudden, clandestine decision to station strategic weapons for the first time outside of Soviet soil-- is a deliberately provocative and unjustified change in the status quo which cannot be accepted by this country, if our courage and our commitments are ever to be trusted again by either friend or foe.

The 1930's taught us a clear lesson: aggressive conduct, if allowed to go unchecked and unchallenged ultimately leads to war. This nation is opposed to war. We are also true to our word. Our unswerving objective, therefore, must be to prevent the use of these missiles against this or any other country, and to secure their withdrawal or elimination from the Western Hemisphere.

Our policy has been one of patience and restraint, as befits a peaceful and powerful nation, which leads a worldwide alliance. We have been determined not to be diverted from our central concerns by mere irritants and fanatics. But now further action is required-- and it is under way; and these actions may only be the beginning. We will not prematurely or unnecessarily risk the costs of worldwide nuclear war in which even the fruits of victory would be ashes in our mouth--but neither will we shrink from that risk at any time it must be faced.

Acting, therefore, in the defense of our own security and of the entire Western Hemisphere, and under the authority entrusted to me by the Constitution as endorsed by the resolution of the Congress, I have directed that the following initial steps be taken immediately:

First: To halt this offensive buildup, a strict quarantine on all offensive military equipment under shipment to Cuba is being initiated. All ships of any kind bound for Cuba from whatever nation or port will, if found to contain cargoes of offensive weapons, be turned back. This quarantine will be extended, if needed, to other types of cargo and carriers. We are not at this time, however, denying the necessities of life as the Soviets attempted to do in their Berlin blockade of 1948.

Second: I have directed the continued and increased close surveillance of Cuba and its military buildup. The foreign ministers of the OAS, in their communique of October 6, rejected secrecy in such matters in this hemisphere. Should these offensive military preparations continue, thus increasing the threat to the hemisphere, further action will be justified. I have directed the Armed Forces to prepare for any eventualities; and I trust that in the interest of both the Cuban people and the Soviet technicians at the sites, the hazards to all concerned in continuing this threat will be recognized.

Third: It shall be the policy of this Nation to regard any nuclear missile launched from Cuba against any nation in the Western Hemisphere as an attack by the Soviet Union on the United States, requiring a full retaliatory response upon the Soviet Union.

Fourth: As a necessary military precaution, I have reinforced our base at Guantanamo, evacuated today the dependents of our personnel there, and ordered additional military units to be on a standby alert basis.

Fifth: We are calling tonight for an immediate meeting of the Organ of Consultation under the Organization of American States, to consider this threat to hemispheric security and to invoke articles 6 and 8 of the Rio Treaty in support of all necessary action. The United Nations Charter allows for regional security arrangements-- and the nations of this hemisphere decided long ago against the military presence of outside powers. Our other allies around the world have also been alerted.

Sixth: Under the Charter of the United Nations, we are asking tonight that an emergency meeting of the Security Council be convoked without delay to take action against this latest Soviet threat to world peace. Our resolution will call for the prompt dismantling and withdrawal of all offensive weapons in Cuba, under the supervision of U.N. observers, before the quarantine can be lifted.

Seventh and finally: I call upon Chairman Khrushchev to halt and eliminate this clandestine, reckless and provocative threat to world peace and to stable relations between our two nations. I call upon him further to abandon this course of world domination, and to join in an historic effort to end the perilous arms race and to transform the history of man. He has an opportunity now to move the world back from the abyss of destruction--by returning to his government's own words that it had no need to station missiles outside its own territory, and withdrawing these weapons from Cuba--by refraining from any action which will widen or deepen the present crisis--and then by participating in a search for peaceful and permanent solutions.

This Nation is prepared to present its case against the Soviet threat to peace, and our own proposals for a peaceful world, at any time and in any forum--in the OAS, in the United Nations, or in any other meeting that could be useful--without limiting our freedom of action. We have in the past made strenuous efforts to limit the spread of nuclear weapons. We have proposed the elimination of all arms and military bases in a fair and effective disarmament treaty. We are prepared to discuss new proposals for the removal of tensions on both sides--including the possibility of a genuinely independent Cuba, free to determine its own destiny. We have no wish to war with the Soviet Union--for we are a peaceful people who desire to live in peace with all other peoples.

But it is difficult to settle or even discuss these problems in an atmosphere of intimidation. That is why this latest Soviet threat--or any other threat which is made either independently or in response to our actions this week--must and will be met with determination. Any hostile move anywhere in the world against the safety and freedom of peoples to whom we are committed--including in particular the brave people of West Berlin--will be met by whatever action is needed.

Finally, I want to say a few words to the captive people of Cuba, to whom this speech is being directly carried by special radio facilities.

I speak to you as a friend, as one who knows of your deep attachment to your fatherland, as one who shares your aspirations for liberty and justice for all. And I have watched and the American people have watched with deep sorrow how your nationalist revolution was betrayed-- and how your fatherland fell under foreign domination. Now your leaders are no longer Cuban leaders inspired by Cuban ideals. They are puppets and agents of an international conspiracy which has turned Cuba against your friends and neighbors in the Americas--and turned it into the first Latin American country to become a target for nuclear war--the first Latin American country to have these weapons on its soil.

These new weapons are not in your interest. They contribute nothing to your peace and well-being. They can only undermine it. But this country has no wish to cause you to suffer or to impose any system upon you. We know that your lives and land are being used as pawns by those who deny your freedom.

Many times in the past, the Cuban people have risen to throw out tyrants who destroyed their liberty. And I have no doubt that most Cubans today look forward to the time when they will be truly free--free from foreign domination, free to choose their own leaders, free to select their own system, free to own their own land, free to speak and write and worship without fear or degradation. And then shall Cuba be welcomed back to the society of free nations and to the associations of this hemisphere.

My fellow citizens: let no one doubt that this is a difficult and dangerous effort on which we have set out. No one can see precisely what course it will take or what costs or casualties will be incurred. Many months of sacrifice and self-discipline lie ahead--months in which our patience and our will will be tested--months in which many threats and denunciations will keep us aware of our dangers. But the greatest danger of all would be to do nothing.

The path we have chosen for the present is full of hazards, as all paths are--but it is the one most consistent with our character and courage as a nation and our commitments around the world. The cost of freedom is always high--and Americans have always paid it. And one path we shall never choose, and that is the path of surrender or submission.

Our goal is not the victory of might, but the vindication of right- - not peace at the expense of freedom, but both peace and freedom, here in this hemisphere, and, we hope, around the world. God willing, that goal will be achieved.

Thank you and good night.

The "I am a Berliner" Speech

June 26, 1963
Rudolph Wilde Platz, Berlin, Germany

I am proud to come to this city as the guest of your distinguished Mayor, who has symbolized throughout the world the fighting spirit of West Berlin. And I am proud to visit the Federal Republic with your distinguished Chancellor who for so many years has committed Germany to democracy and freedom and progress, and to come here in the company of my fellow American, General Clay, who has been in this city during its great moments of crisis and will come again if ever needed.

Two thousand years ago the proudest boast was "civis Romanus sum." Today, in the world of freedom, the proudest boast is "Ich bin ein Berliner."

I appreciate my interpreter translating my German!

There are many people in the world who really don't understand, or say they don't, what is the great issue between the free world and the Communist world. Let them come to Berlin. There are some who say that communism is the wave of the future. Let them come to Berlin. And there are some who say in Europe and elsewhere we can work with the Communists. Let them come to Berlin. And there are even a few who say that it is true that communism is an evil system, but it permits us to make economic progress. Lass' sie nach Berlin kommen. Let them come to Berlin.

Freedom has many difficulties and democracy is not perfect, but we have never had to put a wall up to keep our people in, to prevent them from leaving us. I want to say, on behalf of my countrymen, who live many miles away on the other side of the Atlantic, who are far distant from you, that they take the greatest pride that they have been able to share with you, even from a distance, the story of the last 18 years. I know of no town, no city, that has been besieged for 18 years that still lives with the vitality and the force, and the hope and the determination of the city of West Berlin. While the wall is the most obvious and vivid demonstration of the failures of the Communist system, for all the world to see, we take no satisfaction in it, for it is, as your Mayor has said, an offense not only against history but an offense against humanity, separating families, dividing husbands and wives and brothers and sisters, and dividing a people who wish to be joined together.

What is true of this city is true of Germany--real, lasting peace in Europe can never be assured as long as one German out of four is denied the elementary right of free men, and that is to make a free choice. In 18 years of peace and good faith, this generation of Germans has earned the right to be free, including the right to unite their families and their nation in lasting peace, with good will to all people. You live in a defended island of freedom, but your life is part of the main. So let me ask you as I close, to lift your eyes beyond the dangers of today, to the hopes of tomorrow, beyond the freedom merely of this city of Berlin, or your country of Germany, to the advance of freedom everywhere, beyond the wall to the day of peace with justice, beyond yourselves and ourselves to all mankind.

Freedom is indivisible, and when one man is enslaved, all are not free. When all are free, then we can look forward to that day when this city will be joined as one and this country and this great Continent of Europe in a peaceful and hopeful globe. When that day finally comes, as it will, the people of West Berlin can take sober satisfaction in the fact that they were in the front lines for almost two decades.

All free men, wherever they may live, are citizens of Berlin, and, therefore, as a free man, I take pride in the words "Ich bin ein Berliner."

United States Naval Academy Address

August 1, 1963

United States Naval Academy, Annapolis, Maryland

Admiral, officers, members of the Brigade: I hope you will stand at ease. Perhaps the plebes will. Did you explain that to them? That comes later in the course.

I want to express our very strong appreciation to all those of you in the plebe class who have come into the Navy. I hope that you realize how great is the dependence of our country upon the men who serve in our Armed Forces. I sometimes think that the people of this country do not appreciate how secure we are because of the devotion of the men and their wives and children who serve this country in far off places, in the sea, in the air, and on the ground, thousands and thousands of miles away from this country, who make it possible for us all to live in peace each day.

This country owes the greatest debt to our servicemen. In time of war, of course, there is a tremendous enthusiasm and outburst of popular feeling about those who fight and lead our wars, but it is sometimes different in peace. But I can assure the people of this country, from my own personal experience in the last 2 1/2 years, that more than anything, more than anything, the fact that this country is secure and at peace, the fact that dozens of countries allied with us are free and at peace, has been due to the military strength of the United States. And that strength has been directly due to the men who serve in our Armed Forces. So even though it may be at peace, in fact most especially because it is at peace, I take this opportunity to express our appreciation to all of them whether they are here at Annapolis, or whether they are out of sight of land, or underneath the sea.

I want to express our strong hope that all of you who have come to the Academy as plebes will stay with the Navy. I can think of no more rewarding a career. You will have a chance in the next 10, 20, and 30 years to serve the cause of freedom and your country all over the globe, to hold positions of the highest responsibility, to recognize that upon your good judgment in many cases may well rest not only the well-being of the men with whom you serve, but also in a very real sense the security of your country.

I can imagine a no more rewarding career. And any man who may be asked in this century what he did to make his life worth while, I think can respond with a good deal of pride and satisfaction: "I served in the United States Navy." So I congratulate you all. This is a hard job, particularly now as you make the change, but I think it develops in you those qualities which we like to see in our country, which we take pride in. I am sure you are going to stay with it. I am sure you are going to be able, by what you are now going through, to find the means to command others.

So I express our very best wishes to you and tell you that though you will be serving in the Navy in the days when most of those who hold public office have long gone from it, I can assure you in 1963 that your services are needed, that your opportunities are unlimited, and that if I were a young man in 1963 I can imagine no place to be better than right here at this Academy, or at West Point, or in the Air Force, or in some other place beginning a career of service to the United States.

There is an old story-which I will close with which will give you very valuable advice as you follow a naval career-about a young yeoman who watched a lieutenant begin a meteoric career in the Navy, and he always used to go into his office every morning and go to his drawer and take out a piece of paper and look at it. He became the youngest captain, the youngest admiral, the youngest commander-in-chief. Finally one day he had a heart attack. The yeoman said, "I want to see what is in that paper. It might help me." So he went over and opened up the safe and pulled out the paper. And it said, "Left-port; right-starboard."

If you can remember that, your careers are assured!

Thank you.

The Protestant Council Address

November 8, 1963
New York, New York

Dr. Kinsolving, Dr. Sockman, Rev. Potter, Father Morgan, Rabbi Rosenblum, Mr. Mayor, Governor Stevenson, Mr. Champion, Mr. Leidesdorf, distinguished guests, ladies and gentlemen:

I had wondered what I would do when I retired from the Presidency, whenever that time might come, but Dr. Sockman was the first man to suggest work as challenging as the Presidency in becoming chairman of the Protestant Council's annual dinner, and I am very grateful to him.

I also regret very much that another honored guest of this dinner on a previous occasion is not with us tonight. I follow his career with more interest than he might imagine. In his quest for the Presidency, Governor Rockefeller follows the example of other distinguished New Yorkers-Wendell Willkie, Thomas Dewey, Richard Nixon, and I wish him some margin of success.

I am gratified to receive this award from the Council, and I am impressed by what you are doing here in the city, and I think that the words of Reverend Potter bear very careful reflection by us all. The United States is not in the position which England was when Benjamin Disraeli described it as: two nations divided, the rich and the poor. This is generally a prosperous country, but there is a stream of poverty that runs across the United States which is not exposed to the lives of a good many of us and, therefore, we are relatively unaware of it except statistically. It is concentrated to a large measure in the large cities from which, as he said, so many people are moving out. It is concentrated in some of our rural areas.

The New York Times two weeks ago, I think, had an article by Mr. Bigart on desperate poverty in several rural counties of eastern

Kentucky-schools which were without windows, sometimes with occasional teachers, counties without resources to distribute the surplus food that we make available. And what is true in some of the older coal mining areas of the United States is very true in our cities. We see it in some of our statistics, where we have a mental retardation rate for our children of three times that of Sweden, where we have an infant mortality rate behind half the countries of Europe, plus we have about 8 million boys and girls in this decade who will drop out of school, and a good many of them out of work. And this Council, and the religious leaders of the Catholic faith and Jewish faith have a great responsibility not only for the moral life of the community, but also for the well-being of those who have been left behind.

We are attempting, in cooperation with the State and the city, as Reverend Potter described, to carry out a pilot program here in the city of New York, but it is only a beginning, and there are hundreds of thousands without resources, and we have a responsibility to all of them. We have it in Washington. Schools were integrated a few years ago. About half the population of Washington is Negro. Today about 85 percent of the children in the schools of Washington are Negro. Other whites who are more prosperous generally have moved away and left the problem behind. So I commend this council for its concern for the Family of Man here in the city of New York, and I hope its efforts will be matched by others in other cities across the country, and that we will remember in this very rich, constantly increasing prosperity that there are some for whom we have a responsibility.

I want to speak tonight very briefly, however, about the Family of Man beyond the United States. Just as the Family of Man is not limited to a single race or religion, neither can it be limited to a single city or country. The Family of Man is more than 3 billion strong. It lives in more than 100 nations. Most of its members are not white. Most of them are not Christians. Most of them know nothing about free enterprise or due process of law or the Australian ballot.

If our society is to promote the Family of Man, let us realize the magnitude of our task. This is a sobering assignment. For the Family of Man in the world of today is not faring very well.

The members of a family should be at peace with one another, but they are not. And the hostilities are not confined to the great powers of the East and the West. On the contrary, the United States and the Soviet Union, each fully aware of their mutually destructive powers and their worldwide responsibilities and obligations, have on occasion sought to introduce a greater note of caution in their approach to areas of conflict.

Yet lasting peace between East and West would not bring peace to the Family of Man. Within the last month, the last four weeks, the world has witnessed active or threatened hostilities in a dozen or more disputes independent of the struggle between communism and the free world-disputes between Africans and Europeans in Angola, between North African neighbors in the Maghreb, between two Arab states over Yemen, between India and Pakistan, between Indonesia and Malaysia, Cambodia and Viet-Nam, Ethiopia and Somalia, and a long list of others.

In each of these cases of conflict, neither party can afford to divert to these needless hostilities the precious resources that their people require. In almost every case, the parties to these disputes have more in common ethnically and ideologically than do the Soviet Union and the United States-yet they often seem less able and less willing to get together and negotiate. In almost every case, their continuing conflict invites outside intervention and threatens worldwide escalation-yet the major powers are hard put to limit events in these areas.

As I said recently at the United Nations, even little wars are dangerous in this nuclear world. The long labor of peace is an under taking for every nation, large and small, for every member of the Family of Man. "In this effort none of us can remain unaligned. To this goal none can be uncommitted." If the Family of Man cannot achieve greater unity and harmony, the very planet which serves as its home may find its future in peril.

But there are other troubles besetting the human family. Many of its members live in poverty and misery and despair. More than one out of three, according to the FAO, suffers from malnutrition or under-nutrition or both-while more than one in ten live "below the breadline." Two out of every five adults on this planet are, according to UNESCO, illiterate. One out of eight suffers from trachoma or lives in an area where malaria is still a clear and present danger. Ten million-nearly as many men, women, and children as inhabit this city and Los Angeles combined-still suffer from leprosy; and countless others suffer from yaws or tuberculosis or intestinal parasites.

For the blessings of life have not been distributed evenly to the Family of Man. Life expectancy in this most fortunate of nations has reached the Biblical 3 score years and 10; but in the less developed nations of Africa, Asia, and Latin America, the overwhelming majority of infants cannot expect to live even 2 score years and 5. In those vast continents, more than half of the children of primary school age are not in school. More than half the families live in substandard dwellings. More than half the people live on less than $100 a year. Two out of every three adults are illiterate.

The Family of Man can survive differences of race and religion. Contrary to the assertions of Mr. Khrushchev, it can accept differences of ideology, politics, and economics. But it cannot survive, in the form in which we know it, a nuclear war-and neither can it long endure the growing gulf between the rich and the poor.

The rich must help the poor. The industrialized nations must help the developing nations. And the United States, along with its allies, must do better-not worse-by its foreign aid program, which is now being subjected to such intense debate in the Senate of the United States.

Too often we advance the need of foreign aid only in terms of our economic self-interest. To be sure, foreign aid is in our economic self-interest. It provides more than a half a million jobs for workers in every State. It finances a rising share of our exports and builds new and growing export markets. It generates the purchase of military and civilian equipment by other governments in this country. It makes possible the stationing of 3 1/2 million troops along the Communist periphery at a price one-tenth the cost of maintaining a comparable number of American soldiers. And it helps to stave off the kind of chaos or Communist takeover or Communist attack that would surely demand our critical and costly attention. The Korean conflict alone, forgetting for a moment the thousands of Americans who lost their lives, cost four times as much as our total world-wide aid budget for the current year.

But foreign aid is not advanced only out of American economic self-interest. The gulf between rich and poor which divides the Family of Man is an invitation to agitators, subversives, and aggressors. It encourages the ambitions of those who desire to dominate the world, which threatens the peace and freedom of us all.

"Never has there been any question in my mind," President Eisenhower said recently, "as to the necessity of a program of economic and military aid to keep the free nations of the world from being overrun by the Communists. It is that simple."

This is not a partisan matter. For 17 years, through three administrations, this program has been supported by Presidents and leaders of both parties. It is being supported today in the Congress by those in leadership on both sides of the aisle who recognize the urgency of this program in the achievement of peace and freedom. Yet there are still those who are unable or unwilling to accept these simple facts-who find it politically convenient to denounce foreign aid on the one hand, and in the same sentence to denounce the Communist menace. I do not say that there have been no mistakes in aid administration. I do not say it has purchased for us lasting popularity or servile satellites. I do say it is one essential instrument in the creation of a better, more peaceful world. I do say that it has substituted strength for weakness all over the globe, encouraging nations struggling to be free to stand on their own two feet. And I do not say that merely because others may not bear their share of the burden that it is any excuse for the United States not to meet its responsibility.

To those who say it has been a failure, how can we measure success-by the economic viability of 14 nations in Western Europe, Japan, Spain, Lebanon, where our economic aid, after having completed its task, has ended; by the refusal of a single one of the more than 50 new members of the United Nations to go the Communist route; by the reduction of malaria in India, for example, from 75 million cases to 2,000; by the 18,000 classrooms and 4 million textbooks bringing learning to Latin America under the infant Alliance for Progress?

Nearly two years ago my wife and I visited Bogotá, Colombia, where a vast new Alliance for Progress housing project was just getting under way. Earlier this year I received a letter from the first resident of this 1200 new home development. "Now," he wrote, "we have dignity and liberty."

Dignity and liberty-these words are the foundation, as they have been since '47, of the mutual security program. For the dignity and liberty of all free men, of a world of diversity where the balance of power is clearly on the side of free nations, is essential to the security of the United States. And to weaken and water down the pending program, to confuse and confine its flexibility with rigid restrictions and rejections, will not only harm our economy, it will hamper our security. It will waste our present investment and it will, above all, forfeit our obligation to our fellow man, obligations that stem from our wealth and strength, from our devotion to freedom and from our membership in the Family of Man.

I think we can meet those obligations. I think we can afford to fulfill these commitments around the world when 90 percent of them are used to purchase goods and services here in the United States, including, for example, one-third of this Nation's total fertilizer exports, one-fourth of our iron and steel exports around the world, one-third of our locomotive exports. A cut of $1 billion in our total foreign aid program may save $100 million in our balance of payments-but it costs us $900 million in exports.

I think the American people are willing to shoulder this burden. Contrary to repeated warnings, prophecies, and expressions of hope, in the 17 years since the Marshall plan began, I know of no single officeholder who was ever defeated because he supported this program, and the burden is less today than ever before. Despite the fact that this year's AID request is about $1 billion less than the average request of the last 15 years, many Members of Congress today complain that 4 percent of our Federal budget is too much to devote to foreign aid-yet in 1951 that program amounted to nearly 20 percent of our budget-20 percent in 1951, and 4 percent today. They refuse today to vote more than $4 billion to this effort-yet in 1951 when this country was not nearly as well off, the Congress voted $8 billion to the same cause. They are fearful today of the effects of sending to other people seven-tenths of 1 percent of our gross national product-but in 1951 we devoted nearly four times that proportion to this purpose, and concentrated in a very limited area, unlike today when our obligations stretch around the globe.

This Congress has already reduced this year's aid budget $600 million below the amount recommended by the Clay committee. Is this Nation stating it cannot afford to spend an additional $600 million to help the developing nations of the world become strong and free and independent-an amount less than this country's annual outlay for lipstick, face cream, and chewing gum? Are we saying that we cannot help 19 needy neighbors in Latin America and do as much for the 19 as the Communist bloc is doing for the Island of Cuba alone?

Some say that they are tiring of this task, or tired of world problems and their complexities, or tired of hearing those who receive our aid disagree with us. But are we tired of living in a free world? Do we expect that world overnight to be like the United States? Are we going to stop now merely because we have not produced complete success?

I do not believe our adversaries are tired and I cannot believe that the United States of America in 1963 is fatigued.

Surely the Americans of the 1960s can do half as well as the Americans of the 1950s. Surely we are not going to throw away our hopes and means for peaceful progress in an outburst of irritation and frustration. I do not want it said of us what T. S. Eliot said of others some years ago: "These were a decent people. Their only monument: the asphalt road and a thousand lost golf balls." I think we can do better than that.

My fellow Americans, I hope we will be guided by our interests. I hope we will recognize that the struggle is by no means over; that it is essential that we not only maintain our effort, but that we persevere; that we not only endure, in Mr. Faulkner's words, but also prevail. It is essential, in short, that the word go forth from the United States to all who are concerned about the future of the Family of Man; that we are not weary in well-doing. And we shall, I am confident, if we maintain the pace, we shall in due season reap the kind of world we deserve and deserve the kind of world we will have.

Thank you.

His Last Public Address

November 21, 1963
San Antonio, Texas

Mr. Secretary, Governor, Mr. Vice President, Senator, Members of the Congress, members of the military, ladies and gentlemen:

For more than 3 years I have spoken about the New Frontier. This is not a partisan term, and it is not the exclusive property of Republicans or Democrats. It refers, instead, to this Nation's place in history, to the fact that we do stand on the edge of a great new era, filled with both crisis and opportunity, an era to be characterized by achievement and by challenge. It is an era which calls for action and for the best efforts of all those who would test the unknown and the uncertain in every phase of human endeavor. It is a time for pathfinders and pioneers.

I have come to Texas today to salute an outstanding group of pioneers, the men who man the Brooks Air Force Base School of Aerospace Medicine and the Aerospace Medical Center. It is fitting that San Antonio should be the site of this center and this school as we gather to dedicate this complex of buildings. For this city has long been the home of the pioneers in the air. It was here that Sidney Brooks, whose memory we honor today, was born and raised. It was here that Charles Lindbergh and Claire Chennault, and a host of others, who, in World War I and World War II and Korea, and even today have helped demonstrate American mastery of the skies, trained at Kelly Field and Randolph Field, which form a major part of aviation history. And in the new frontier of outer space, while headlines may be made by others in other places, history is being made every day by the men and women of the Aerospace Medical Center, without whom there could be no history.

Many Americans make the mistake of assuming that space research has no values here on earth. Nothing could be further from the truth. Just as the wartime development of radar gave us the transistor, and all that it made possible, so research in space medicine holds the promise of substantial benefit for those of us who are earthbound. For our effort in space is not as some have suggested, a competitor for the natural resources that we need to develop the earth. It is a working partner and a coproducer of these resources. And nothing makes this clearer than the fact that medicine in space is going to make our lives healthier and happier here on earth.

I give you three examples: first, medical space research may open up new understanding of man's relation to his environment. Examinations of the astronaut's physical, and mental, and emotional reactions can teach us more about the differences between normal and abnormal, about the causes and effects of disorientation, about changes in metabolism which could result in extending the life span. When you study the effects on our astronauts of exhaust gases which can contaminate their environment, and you seek ways to alter these gases so as to reduce their toxicity, you are working on problems similar to those in our great urban centers which themselves are being corrupted by gases and which must be clear.

And second, medical space research may revolutionize the technology and the techniques of modern medicine. Whatever new devices are created, for example, to monitor our astronauts, to measure their heart activity, their breathing, their brain waves, their eye motion, at great distances and under difficult conditions, will also represent a major advance in general medical instrumentation. Heart patients may even be able to wear a light monitor which will sound a warning if their activity exceeds certain limits. An instrument recently developed to record automatically the impact of acceleration upon an astronaut's eyes will also be of help to small children who are suffering miserably from eye defects, but are unable to describe their impairment. And also by the use of instruments similar to those used in Project Mercury, this Nation's private as well as public nursing services are being improved, enabling one nurse now to give more critically ill patients greater attention than they ever could in the past.

And third, medical space research may lead to new safeguards against hazards common to many environments. Specifically, our astronauts will need fundamentally new devices to protect them from the ill effects of radiation which can have a profound influence upon medicine and man's relations to our present environment.

Here at this center we have the laboratories, the talent, the resources to give new impetus to vital research in the life centers. I am not suggesting that the entire space program is justified alone by what is done in medicine. The space program stands on its own as a contribution to national strength. And last Saturday at Cape Canaveral I saw our new Saturn C-1 rocket booster, which, with its payload, when it rises in December of this year, will be, for the first time, the largest booster in the world, carrying into space the largest payload that any country in the world has ever sent into space.

I think the United States should be a leader. A country as rich and powerful as this which bears so many burdens and responsibilities, which has so many opportunities, should be second to none. And in December, while I do not regard our mastery of space as anywhere near complete, while I recognize that there are still areas where we are behind--at least in one area, the size of the booster--this year I hope the United States will be ahead. And I am for it. We have a long way to go. Many weeks and months and years of long, tedious work lie ahead. There will be setbacks and frustrations and disappointments. There will be, as there always are, pressures in this country to do less in this area as in so many others, and temptations to do something else that is perhaps easier. But this research here must go on. This space effort must go on. The conquest of space must and will go ahead. That much we know. That much we can say with confidence and conviction.

Frank O'Connor, the Irish writer, tells in one of his books how, as a boy, he and his friends would make their way across the countryside, and when they came to an orchard wall that seemed too high and too doubtful to try and too difficult to permit their voyage to continue, they took off their hats and tossed them over the wall--and then they had no choice but to follow them.

This Nation has tossed its cap over the wall of space, and we have no choice but to follow it. Whatever the difficulties, they will be overcome. Whatever the hazards, they must be guarded against. With the vital help of this Aerospace Medical Center, with the help of all those who labor in the space endeavor, with the help and support of all Americans, we will climb this wall with safety and with speed-and we shall then explore the wonders on the other side.

Thank you.

The Undelivered Speech

The Watchman Speech [Undelivered]

November 22, 1963
Dallas, Texas

I am honored to have this invitation to address the annual meeting of the Dallas Citizens Council, joined by the members of the Dallas Assembly--and pleased to have this opportunity to salute the Graduate Research Center of the Southwest.

It is fitting that these two symbols of Dallas progress are united in the sponsorship of this meeting. For they represent the best qualities, I am told, of leadership and learning in this city--and leadership and learning are indispensable to each other. The advancement of learning depends on community leadership for financial and political support and the products of that learning, in turn, are essential to the leadership's hopes for continued progress and prosperity. It is not a coincidence that those communities possessing the best in research and graduate facilities--from MIT to Cal Tech--tend to attract the new and growing industries. I congratulate those of you here in Dallas who have recognized these basic facts through the creation of the unique and forward-looking Graduate Research Center.

This link between leadership and learning is not only essential at the community level. It is even more indispensable in world affairs. Ignorance and misinformation can handicap the progress of a city or a company, but they can, if allowed to prevail in foreign policy, handicap this country's security. In a world of complex and continuing problems, in a world full of frustrations and irritations, America's leadership must be guided by the lights of learning and reason or else those who confuse rhetoric with reality and the plausible with the possible will gain the popular ascendancy with their seemingly swift and simple solutions to every world problem.

There will always be dissident voices heard in the land, expressing opposition without alternatives, finding fault but never favor, perceiving gloom on every side and seeking influence without responsibility. Those voices are inevitable.

But today other voices are heard in the land--voices preaching doctrines wholly unrelated to reality, wholly unsuited to the sixties, doctrines which apparently assume that words will suffice without weapons, that vituperation is as good as victory and that peace is a sign of weakness. At a time when the national debt is steadily being reduced in terms of its burden on our economy, they see that debt as the greatest single threat to our security. At a time when we are steadily reducing the number of Federal employees serving every thousand citizens, they fear those supposed hordes of civil servants far more than the actual hordes of opposing armies.

We cannot expect that everyone, to use the phrase of a decade ago, will "talk sense to the American people." But we can hope that fewer people will listen to nonsense. And the notion that this Nation is headed for defeat through deficit, or that strength is but a matter of slogans, is nothing but just plain nonsense.

I want to discuss with you today the status of our strength and our security because this question clearly calls for the most responsible qualities of leadership and the most enlightened products of scholarship. For this Nation's strength and security are not easily or cheaply obtained, nor are they quickly and simply explained. There are many kinds of strength and no one kind will suffice. Overwhelming nuclear strength cannot stop a guerrilla war. Formal pacts of alliance cannot stop internal subversion. Displays of material wealth cannot stop the disillusionment of diplomats subjected to discrimination.

Above all, words alone are not enough. The United States is a peaceful nation. And where our strength and determination are clear, our words need merely to convey conviction, not belligerence. If we are strong, our strength will speak for itself. If we are weak, words will be of no help.

I realize that this Nation often tends to identify turning-points in world affairs with the major addresses which preceded them. But it was not the Monroe Doctrine that kept all Europe away from this hemisphere--it was the strength of the British fleet and the width of the Atlantic Ocean. It was not General Marshall's speech at Harvard which kept communism out of Western Europe--it was the strength and stability made possible by our military and economic assistance.

In this administration also it has been necessary at times to issue specific warnings--warnings that we could not stand by and watch the Communists conquer Laos by force, or intervene in the Congo, or swallow West Berlin, or maintain offensive missiles on Cuba. But while our goals were at least temporarily obtained in these and other instances, our successful defense of freedom was due not to the words we used, but to the strength we stood ready to use on behalf of the principles we stand ready to defend.

This strength is composed of many different elements, ranging from the most massive deterrents to the most subtle influences. And all types of strength are needed--no one kind could do the job alone. Let us take a moment, therefore, to review this Nation's progress in each major area of strength.

I.

First, as Secretary McNamara made clear in his address last Monday, the strategic nuclear power of the United States has been so greatly modernized and expanded in the last 1,000 days, by the rapid production and deployment of the most modern missile systems, that any and all potential aggressors are clearly confronted now with the impossibility of strategic victory--and the certainty of total destruction--if by reckless attack they should ever force upon us the necessity of a strategic reply.

In less than 3 years, we have increased by 50 percent the number of Polaris submarines scheduled to be in force by the next fiscal year, increased by more than 70 percent our total Polaris purchase program, increased by more than 75 percent our Minuteman purchase program, increased by 50 percent the portion of our strategic bombers on 15-minute alert, and increased by too percent the total number of nuclear weapons available in our strategic alert forces. Our security is further enhanced by the steps we have taken regarding these weapons to improve the speed and certainty of their response, their readiness at all times to respond, their ability to survive an attack, and their ability to be carefully controlled and directed through secure command operations.

II.

But the lessons of the last decade have taught us that freedom cannot be defended by strategic nuclear power alone. We have, therefore, in the last 3 years accelerated the development and deployment of tactical nuclear weapons, and increased by 60 percent the tactical nuclear forces deployed in Western Europe.

Nor can Europe or any other continent rely on nuclear forces alone, whether they are strategic or tactical. We have radically improved the readiness of our conventional forces--increased by 45 percent the number of combat ready Army divisions, increased by 100 percent the procurement of modern Army weapons and equipment, increased by 100 percent our ship construction, conversion, and modernization program, increased by too percent our procurement of tactical aircraft, increased by 30 percent the number of tactical air squadrons, and increased the strength of the Marines. As last month's "Operation Big Lift"--which originated here in Texas--showed so clearly, this Nation is prepared as never before to move substantial numbers of men in surprisingly little time to advanced positions anywhere in the world. We have increased by 175 percent the procurement of airlift aircraft, and we have already achieved a 75 percent increase in our existing strategic airlift capability. Finally, moving beyond the traditional roles of our military forces, we have achieved an increase of nearly 600 percent in our special forces--those forces that are prepared to work with our allies and friends against the guerrillas, saboteurs, insurgents and assassins who threaten freedom in a less direct but equally dangerous manner.

III.

But American military might should not and need not stand alone against the ambitions of international communism. Our security and strength, in the last analysis, directly depend on the security and strength of others, and that is why our military and economic assistance plays such a key role in enabling those who live on the periphery of the Communist world to maintain their independence of choice. Our assistance to these nations can be painful, risky and costly, as is true in Southeast Asia today. But we dare not weary of the task. For our assistance makes possible the stationing of 3-5 million allied troops along the Communist frontier at one-tenth the cost of maintaining a comparable number of American soldiers. A successful Communist breakthrough in these areas, necessitating direct United States intervention, would cost us several times as much as our entire foreign aid program, and might cost us heavily in American lives as well.

About 70 percent of our military assistance goes to nine key countries located on or near the borders of the Communist bloc-- nine countries confronted directly or indirectly with the threat of Communist aggression--Viet-Nam, Free China, Korea, India, Pakistan, Thailand, Greece, Turkey, and Iran. No one of these countries possesses on its own the resources to maintain the forces which our own Chiefs of Staff think needed in the common interest. Reducing our efforts to train, equip, and assist their armies can only encourage Communist penetration and require in time the increased overseas deployment of American combat forces. And reducing the economic help needed to bolster these nations that undertake to help defend freedom can have the same disastrous result. In short, the $50 billion we spend each year on our own defense could well be ineffective without the $4 billion required for military and economic assistance.

Our foreign aid program is not growing in size, it is, on the contrary, smaller now than in previous years. It has had its weaknesses, but we have undertaken to correct them. And the proper way of treating weaknesses is to replace them with strength, not to increase those weaknesses by emasculating essential programs. Dollar for dollar, in or out of government, there is no better form of investment in our national security than our much-abused foreign aid program. We cannot afford to lose it. We can afford to maintain it. We can surely afford, for example, to do as much for our 19 needy neighbors of Latin America as the Communist bloc is sending to the island of Cuba alone.

IV.

I have spoken of strength largely in terms of the deterrence and resistance of aggression and attack. But, in today's world, freedom can be lost without a shot being fired, by ballots as well as bullets. The success of our leadership is dependent upon respect for our mission in the world as well as our missiles--on a clearer recognition of the virtues of freedom as well as the evils of tyranny.

That is why our Information Agency has doubled the shortwave broadcasting power of the Voice of America and increased the number of broadcasting hours by 30 percent, increased Spanish language broadcasting to Cuba and Latin America from I to 9 hours a day, increased seven-fold to more than 3-5 million copies the number of American books being translated and published for Latin American readers, and taken a host of other steps to carry our message of truth and freedom to all the far corners of the earth.

And that is also why we have regained the initiative in the exploration of outer space, making an annual effort greater than the combined total of all space activities undertaken during the fifties, launching more than 130 vehicles into earth orbit, putting into actual operation valuable weather and communications satellites, and making it clear to all that the United States of America has no intention of finishing second in space.

This effort is expensive--but it pays its own way, for freedom and for America. For there is no longer any fear in the free world that a Communist lead in space will become a permanent assertion of supremacy and the basis of military superiority. There is no longer any doubt about the strength and skill of American science, American industry, American education, and the American free enterprise system. In short, our national space effort represents a great gain in, and a great resource of, our national strength--and both Texas and Texans are contributing greatly to this strength.

Finally, it should be clear by now that a nation can be no stronger abroad than she is at home. Only an America which practices what it preaches about equal rights and social justice will be respected by those whose choice affects our future. Only an America which has fully educated its citizens is fully capable of tackling the complex problems and perceiving the hidden dangers of the world in which we live. And only an America which is growing and prospering economically can sustain the worldwide defenses of freedom, while demonstrating to all concerned the opportunities of our system and society.

It is clear, therefore, that we are strengthening our security as well as our economy by our recent record increases in national income and output--by surging ahead of most of Western Europe in the rate of business expansion and the margin of corporate profits, by maintaining a more stable level of prices than almost any of our overseas competitors, and by cutting personal and corporate income taxes by some $ I I billion, as I have proposed, to assure this Nation of the longest and strongest expansion in our peacetime economic history.

This Nation's total output--which 3 years ago was at the $500 billion mark--will soon pass $600 billion, for a record rise of over $too billion in 3 years. For the first time in history we have 70 million men and women at work. For the first time in history average factory earnings have exceeded $100 a week. For the first time in history corporation profits after taxes--which have risen 43 percent in less than 3 years--have an annual level of $27.4 billion.

My friends and fellow citizens: I cite these facts and figures to make it clear that America today is stronger than ever before. Our adversaries have not abandoned their ambitions, our dangers have not diminished, our vigilance cannot be relaxed. But now we have the military, the scientific, and the economic strength to do whatever must be done for the preservation and promotion of freedom.

That strength will never be used in pursuit of aggressive ambitions-- it will always be used in pursuit of peace. It will never be used to promote provocations--it will always be used to promote the peaceful settlement of disputes.

We in this country, in this generation, are--by destiny rather than choice--the watchmen on the walls of world freedom. We ask, therefore, that we may be worthy of our power and responsibility, that we may exercise our strength with wisdom and restraint, and that we may achieve in our time and for all time the ancient vision of "peace on earth, good will toward men." That must always be our goal, and the righteousness of our cause must always underlie our strength. For as was written long ago: "except the Lord keep the city, the watchman waketh but in vain."

Afterword

Now He Belongs to the Ages

"Now he belongs to the ages."

~ *Secretary of War Edwin M. Stanton,*
Upon the Death of President Lincoln
April 15, 1865

~ * ~

The similarities between Kennedy and Lincoln are fascinating. Kennedy was elected in 1960, Lincoln in 1860. Strangely enough, Lincoln was elected to Congress in 1846, Kennedy in 1946. Both were champions of civil rights and strong supporters of the military. Both were Northerners shot on a Friday, and both were succeeded by Southern presidents named Johnson. The alleged assassins of both men were shot before being tried. Both assassinations were shrouded in accusations of conspiracy. And both Lincoln and Kennedy hold a special place in the history of American Presidents.

But President Kennedy was also unique. A fiscal, tax-cutting conservative and staunch supporter of American military might, Kennedy believed in the God-given talents of a free people and American exceptionalism. It makes you wonder if such a man would ever be welcome in today's Democrat Party, let alone be its standard-bearer.

JFK had a profound influence on my life. Assassinated a month following my own father's death, Kennedy became a surrogate role model for me when it came to believing in the great good that was America. And coincidentally enough, President Kennedy was born in the same year of my father, 1917.

Even during my military career, President Kennedy held a special place in the hearts of my fellow-Airborne Infantry Army officers, and especially those who proudly donned the Green Beret. Kennedy's portrait would often share a place of honor with that of a successor of his, the greatest American president of my lifetime, President Ronald Reagan. Both men were exceptionally gifted inspirational leaders who believed in America!

Their legacy is one worth resurrecting and trumpeting. Now that would be a very American thing to do!

Long may we live and learn! God bless America!

~ Judge Hal Moroz

~ * ~

*"I have set watchmen upon thy walls, O Jerusalem,
which shall never hold their peace day nor night:
ye that make mention of the LORD, keep not silence,
And give him no rest, till he establish,
and till he make Jerusalem a praise in the earth."*

~ *Isaiah 62:6-7*

About the Author

Judge Hal Moroz

"Whether therefore ye eat, or drink, or whatsoever ye do, do all to the glory of God."

~ Psalm 37:23

Hal Moroz is an Attorney and Counselor at Law, who served as a county judge and city chief judge in the great State of Georgia. Judge Moroz has represented individual clients and small, medium and large businesses in a variety of legal matters. And his practice in the law has ranged from small claims courts to the Supreme Court of the United States.

Judge Moroz is also an accomplished soldier and statesman, as well as a retired U.S. Army officer, having served in the Airborne Infantry. Judge Moroz served on the faculty of Florida Coastal School of Law in Jacksonville, Florida, and the State Bar of Georgia's Institute for Continuing Legal Education (ICLE). He is a former candidate for the U.S. Congress, and served as Special Counsel to the Georgia Republican Party's First Congressional District Committee in the 2000 primary and general elections, and went on to serve as a Presidential Ballot Inspector/Observer during the 2000 "recount" in Florida. Following the 2000 election, Judge Moroz was a candidate for federal judgeships in the U.S. District Court for the

Middle District of Florida and the U.S. District Court for the Northern District of Illinois.

Hal Moroz is also a prolific writer, having authored numerous legal articles, weekly legal newspaper columns, and books. Copies of his many books can be ordered at Amazon.com or any major online bookstore!

Hal Moroz can be reached through an internet search
or through his email at: hal@morozlaw.com or his website: MorozLaw.com

~ * ~

Judge Moroz is the founder of the Veterans Law Center, Inc. (VLC), a non-profit, 501(c)(3) charitable organization that serves the interests of America's 24 million military veterans Located on the internet at VeteransLawCenter.org, the Veterans Law Center provides support and counsel to America's honorably discharged veterans, wherever they may be, and they do this free of charge to them.

Judge Moroz Supports the Veterans Law Center!

*If you would like to Support the VLC,
please read the following page ...*

Want to support the Veterans Law Center in its charitable work?

Make a tax-deductible contribution to the Veterans Law Center by

(1) Going online to the **VeteransLawCenter.org**
& clicking **"Donate"**

~ and ~

(2) Whenever you shop online at Amazon, please go to AmazonSmile [https://smile.amazon.com] , name the "Veterans Law Center" as your charity of choice, and place your order, and Amazon will make a contribution to the Veterans Law Center.
It costs you nothing, and Amazon makes the donation!

EIN: 26-1822334

FLORIDA REGISTRATION #: CH29264
A COPY OF THE OFFICIAL REGISTRATION AND FINANCIAL INFORMATION MAY BE OBTAINED FROM THE DIVISION OF CONSUMER SERVICES BY CALLING TOLL-FREE (800-435-7352) WITHIN THE STATE. REGISTRATION DOES NOT IMPLY ENDORSEMENT, APPROVAL, OR RECOMMENDATION BY THE STATE.

www.ingramcontent.com/pod-product-compliance
Lightning Source LLC
Chambersburg PA
CBHW060306290526
45789CB00001B/414